TESTED SENTENCES THAT SELL

TESTED
SENTENCES
THAT SELL

ELMER WHEELER

WWW.TESTEDSELLING.COM

CONTENTS

That Sell Pipe Tobacco

PREFACE

From: Miles Devers,
      Publisher

Dear Friend,

First off, thank you very much for grabbing a copy of this book! You're about to discover how to double your selling power overnight using Elmer Wheeler's tested salesmanship principles.

These methods deliver a knockout punch regardless if you're in business online or offline. In fact, in this "Age of Distraction," *how* you say *what* you say is vital. Not only do you compete with other businesses (or people) in your industry, but, you also compete with the countless distractions your prospects and customers face everyday. If your words don't immediately cut through the static, you're throwing time and money away!

Now that this book is in your hands, invest the time <u>right now</u> to read the first eight chapters. They form the crux of Elmer's tested selling principles.

In Chapter 1, you'll discover why almost everyone gets features and benefits dead-wrong – and – how you can uncover the hidden "sizzles" in your products.

You'll also learn how to harness the power of *Snap Judgments* to sell more without saying more. This powerful method, alone, is responsible for over 150 million Apple iPod sales. It worked in 1937, and it's still going strong today!

And, in Chapter 4 you'll learn my favorite tested selling

method... A principle so powerful – and effective – it makes it almost impossible for your prospects to say "no."

But first...

Why I Want To Give You
7 Free Gifts As Part of
A Rare Experiment

By the time you're done reading this book, your mind will explode with ideas on how to make more money when you apply these principles. But let's be honest with each other... 48-hours from now, you'll forget eighty percent of the ideas you had. Two weeks from now, you'll probably forget all of them.

That's the bad news.

So how do you bridge the gap between *learning* powerful, new ideas and *applying* them?

The good news is, for the first time ever, I'm giving away 7 Free Gifts that will make it easy for you to do just that. They're my way of saying "thank you" for investing in this book.

Simply go to the web address below, right now, to claim your 7 Free Gifts:

www.TestedSelling.com/gifts

If you're not close to a computer, write the web address above in your planner, write it on your hand, leave a voicemail for yourself – do whatever it takes so you'll remember to go to the site ASAP.

They're not "watered-down" bonuses. I could sell them together for $197 or more, but I'm giving them to you for free for two important reasons...

Reason #1 – To Thank You for
Investing in This Book

How many times have you bought something, only to be forgotten or completely unappreciated?

It's a shame, isn't it?

I want your investment in this book to signify the beginning of a prosperous relationship together. That's why I'm taking the first step in investing in *your* success!

I hope you'll get so much value out of these free gifts – and make so much money – that you'll want to invest in other products I have because you get so much bang for your buck. We both win!

And...

Reason #2 – I'm Conducting
A Unique Marketing Experiment

Elmer Wheeler was a fanatical tester. This edition of *Tested Sentences That Sell* wouldn't be a proper tribute if it weren't a marketing experiment, in and of itself.

When you go to **www.TestedSelling.com/gifts,** not only will you get 7 Free Gifts valued at over $197, but you'll also be a part of a unique and historical marketing experiment. One which I'll share the results with you in the future.

So go ahead and claim your 7 Free Gifts right now, then come back and dig into this book.

I cannot tell you what these free gifts are here, but you'll find out when you go to the site. I can only tell you one of them is a unique collector's item.

Don't miss out. Claim your 7 Free Gifts now. Simply go to the web address below.

www.TestedSelling.com/gifts

Once again, I truly appreciate your business and I look forward to sharing Elmer Wheeler's timeless, valuable lessons with you on the following pages of this book.

– Miles Devers

THE STORY BEHIND TESTED SELLING

I learned about this book in 2003 after reading a back-issue of The Gary Halbert Letter. Any book recommended by the late, great "Prince of Print" is a must-have for any serious marketer or copywriter. After constant searching, I found a dirty, ragged copy for $200.

I was hooked from page one. Even though Elmer Wheeler published this book in 1937 – his principles are just as powerful today as they were back then. Technology may evolve and life may get more complex, but human nature stays the same.

His tested selling principles are spelled out in elegantly-simple language using entertaining stories, skits and metaphors. Everyone from top executives to untrained sales representatives can effectively implement his strategies to double, triple, quadruple (or more) sales – by changing just a few words in their sales presentations or sales letters.

Using "Word Magic" Instead of "Magic Words"

Elmer is famous for founding the "Wheeler Word Laboratory." This laboratory embarked on a 10-year study to measure the selling effectiveness of words and sales techniques to determine which formations of words and techniques generate the most sales.

The "Wheeler Word Laboratory" analyzed over 105,000 words and word combinations on over 19,000,000 people. Elmer discovered whenever a salesperson was given a "Tested Selling Sentence" with its proper "Tested Technique" to replace a time-worn statement, more sales followed.

For instance, a single sentence increased sales of a manufacturer's hand lotion at B. Altman's on Fifth Avenue from 60 per week to 927 (mind you – this was in the 1920's!) Imagine if you could boost your sales by 1545% by changing just one sentence!

On another occasion, two "Tested Selling Sentences" completely sold Bloomingdales, Saks 34th Street, Abraham & Straus of Brooklyn, and William Taylor's of Cleveland out of toothbrushes – a staple item – for the first time in the history of those important stores.

It is no surprise this book serves as the ultimate foundation for the success of many marketers and copywriters. Elmer's principles are simple to implement, massively effective and backed by thousands of real-world tests.

So get ready to boost your selling effectiveness by at least 200% in one evening!

CHAPTER 1

DON'T SELL THE STEAK – <u>SELL THE SIZZLE!</u>

(Wheelerpoint 1)

What we mean by the "sizzle" is the BIGGEST selling point in your proposition – the MAIN reasons why your prospects will want to buy. The sizzling of the steak starts the sale more than the cow ever did, though the cow is, of course, very necessary!

Hidden in everything you sell, whether a tangible or an intangible, are "sizzles." Find them and use them to start the sale. Then, after desire is established in the prospect's thinking, you can bring in the necessary technical points.

The good waiter realizes he must sell the bubbles – not the champagne. The grocery clerk sells the pucker – not the pickles, the whiff – not the coffee. It's the tang in the cheese that sells it! The insurance man sells PROTECTION, not cost per week. Only the butcher sells the cow and not the sizzle, yet even he knows that the promise of the sizzle brings him more sales of his better cuts.

For instance, let us take a certain modern vacuum cleaner and see how many "sizzles" we can develop to get the prospect saying "I want!" instead of "Oh hum!":

1. Positive Agitation
2. Time-to-Empty Signal
3. Dirt Finder
4. Automatic Rug Adjuster

1

5. Non-kink Cord
6. Instant Handle Positioner
7. Non-tangle Revolving Brush
8. Grit Removers
9. Lint Removers
10. Dust Removers

These ten big "sizzles" will make people buy this particular make of vacuum cleaner. The construction, the mechanism, and the prices are important, of course, but the "I want" points, as Paul Lewis puts it, are labor-saving, more leisure, cleaner homes, and health.

Therefore, the vacuum cleaner salesman must advise himself:

Don't sell the price tag – sell *fewer backaches!*
Don't sell construction – sell *labor-saving!*
Don't sell the motor – sell *comfort!*
Don't sell ball bearings – sell *ease of operation!*
Don't sell suction – sell *cleaner rugs!*

Health, comfort, labor-saving, leisure, and cleaner homes are the "sizzles" in this particular vacuum cleaner; construction and mechanism the "cow."

Are you beginning to see what is meant by first finding the "sizzles" in what you are selling, before even attempting to form the words to convey the "sizzles" to the prospect?

Put on a pair of "sizzle glasses" now and look at *your own* "sales package." Then write down the one, five, ten, or twenty "sizzles" you find – in the order of what, at first blush, you believe will be of importance to the prospect.

THEN LEARN TO HAVE "YOU-ABILITY"

One BIG QUESTION is running through the prospect's mind as you show your merchandise and tell your sales story, and that question is:

"What will it do for me?"

Therefore, almost everything you say or do must be said and done in such a way that it ALWAYS answers this important question! You must develop a NEED for your product in the mind of the prospect – for until he realizes a need, you will make little sales progress.

Now all of the "sizzles" you list for your product may create a NEED in the mind of the customer – but remember that although these "sizzles" may be of EQUAL IMPORTANCE to you, they may differ in importance to the prospect. If you have "you-ability," you will be able to take your "sizzles" and fit them to each prospect with uncanny accuracy!

"You-ability" is the ability to get on the other side of the fence – to put on a pair of invisible "sizzle glasses" and see your product through the EYES OF THE CUSTOMER. "You-ability" is the ability to say "you," not "I" – and the ability to present the "sizzles" in the order that the CUSTOMER considers important.

SUMMARY OF WHEELERPOINT 1

Buried in every spool of thread, in every row of safety pins, in every automobile, in every insurance policy, in every grocery, in every drug, or in every toilet goods item, are reasons why people will want to buy it.

These big reasons we call the "sizzles."

Before you even start to see your prospects, you must line up, in your own mind, the "sizzles" *they* will consider important. You will then have a "planned presentation," based on all the information you can get about your prospects and your selling package.

You will find that using the word "you" in your sales presentation generates far more results than the word "I."

Being able to say "you" instead of "I" is known as "you-ability."

Remember this first Wheelerpoint: "Don't sell the steak – sell the sizzle." Then with "you-ability" in mind you can convey these "sizzles" to the prospect in the "telegraphic" manner explained in the next chapter.

It's the sizzle that sells the steak – not the cow.

CHAPTER 2

"DON'T WRITE – TELEGRAPH"

(Wheelerpoint 2)

Don't Write – Telegraph means, get the prospect's IMMEDIATE and FAVORABLE attention in the fewest possible words. If you don't make your first message "click," the prospect will leave you mentally, if not physically.

A good sales presentation should use as few words as possible. Any word that does not help to make the sale *endangers* the sale. Therefore, make every word count by using "telegraphic" statements, as there is no time for "letters."

Learn the MAGIC of making your "selling sentences" sell!

HOW TO APPROACH PROSPECTS

People form "snap judgments." They make up their opinions about you in the first ten seconds, and this affects their entire attitude toward what you have to sell them. Give them a brief "telegram" in these first ten seconds so that their opinion will be in your favor. Make the wires "sing" – so you will be given the chance to "follow-up."

I find, after analyzing 105,000 sales words and techniques and noting the results of tests of them on 19,000,000 people, that this is the "magic" used by most star salesmen who make single sentences sell!

For our example of this Wheelerpoint, let me again go back

5

to the vacuum cleaner, and remembering the ten "sizzles" in this cleaner, let us see how we can formulate them into ten-second "telegrams."

"TELEGRAMS" THAT CLICK OPEN PROSPECT'S "MENTAL POCKETBOOKS"

"No other cleaner can use Positive Agitation until 1950."

"The Grit Removers take out dirt you never knew you had."

"You may forget to clean the bag, but the Time-to-Empty Signal won't forget to remind you."

SUMMARY OF WHEELERPOINT 2

A good sales presentation consists of as few words as possible.

If you *hem* and *haw* the "sizzle," you will make few sales, for your prospects will walk away from you or complain that you are high-pressuring them!

YOUR FIRST TEN WORDS ARE MORE IMPORTANT THAN YOUR NEXT TEN THOUSAND!

Therefore, make your FIRST words make FIRST impressions by not STAMMERING and STUTTERING when you face your prospects. They make "snap judgments" of you and the merchandise by "sizing you up" with your first ten words.

First you use judgment in picking the right "sizzle," and then you fit it to the prospect at hand. You dress up the "sizzle" in a ten-second message and practice Wheelerpoint 2, "Don't write – TELEGRAPH."

The technique that goes with what you say will then come

to you naturally and easily, as we shall find in the next Wheelerpoint.

**It's all in what you say
in the first ten seconds.**

CHAPTER 3

"SAY IT WITH FLOWERS"

(Wheelerpoint 3)

Say It With Flowers means PROVE your statements! "Happy returns of the day," when accompanied by flowers, proves you MEAN it!

The flowers in his right hand as he proposes tell her MORE than the mere words from his lips.

You have just ten short seconds and two able hands to sell the prospect – and so you must FORTIFY your words with performance!

You must back up your selling "sizzles" with showmanship!

I do not mean you should be an insincere actor, but I do mean that your words deserve the support of your gestures and facial expressions. Your words will get much better results if SUPPORTED than if left hanging mid-air to themselves, no matter how good the words may be. You know how little the perfunctory "Thank you" of some clerks means to you. It lacks the reinforcement of sincerity.

SYNCHRONIZE YOUR "SIZZLES"
WITH SHOWMANSHIP

Fitting action to your words is the third "earmark" in making a sale "stick" with the prospect.

Talk with your hands? Yes – why not? – if you can use

them in a dignified manner. Gesture with them – keep them busy. Pat them – rub them – move them – start them – stop them! Show them action and you will get action.

Make your prospects SEE – FEEL – TOUCH – HANDLE – almost SMELL and TASTE your sales package and the things they will be heirs to upon placing their approval on the dotted line or their money into your palm!

Make your hands earn a living for you!

HOW TO SELL WITH "FLOWERS"

To keep unity in our examples of these five Wheelerpoints, let me stay with the vacuum cleaner, in illustrating this point. How to apply these same five points to other products will be illustrated in later chapters.

"FLOWERS" THAT GO OVER WITH
VACUUM CLEANER BUYERS

1. Run cleaner under table or into dark corner, point to Dirt Finder, turn switch on and off to dramatize the light and say:

"It sees where to clean – and it's clean where it's been."

2. Step on Automatic Rug Adjuster. Invite prospect to do likewise (monkey-see, monkey-do instinct). Then say:

"It automatically ADJUSTS itself to any thickness of rug."

3. Push cleaner away from you, maintaining your hold on cord. Then pull it back to you lightly, saying:

"It has BALL-BEARING action – a child can move it!"

It's the little things you do as you "speak your lines" that make the sale stand out. The movement of your hands, your head, your feet, and your pencil tells the prospect you are sincere – honest – convincing!

Your face is the prospect's most reliable mirror.

But never, NEVER lose a sale because of an "unprofessional mannerism."

UNPROFESSIONAL MANNERISMS
THAT KILL SALES

"He moved listlessly, pointing aimlessly."

"He leaned on the counter and talked to me and to the next customer."

"He was slow and yawned several times in my face."

"He gazed into space, answering my questions."

"He became antagonized by my many questions."

"He got irritated when I didn't understand quickly."

"His fingernails were shabby; so were his shoes."

"He kept reaching for his order book, trying to high pressure me."

THESE "TELEGRAMS" LACK
ACTION AND DRAMA

"It keeps the home clean." (But how?)

"It's a good investment." (In what way?)

"It's a good buy." (All salesmen say that.)

"You'll like it." (I will?)

"I like it." (So what–?)

WORDS THAT SUGGEST THE PROSPECT
SEE YOUR COMPETITOR

"Listen to me – you just can't go wrong on this."

"Yeah, but theirs is no good."

"I wouldn't depend on what their salesman said."

"I know my business. It don't use up much electricity."

"It's not heavy – I can lift it – see?"

DO YOUR SENTENCES BEGIN
LIKE THIS? – THEN STOP!

"Look..."

"Listen... "

"See..."

"I'm telling you..."

"You see what I mean?"

"Take my word for it."

"Between you and me..."

"Don't let this go any farther, but…"

"COMIC VALENTINE" TECHNIQUES
THAT LOSE SALES

The salesman made three attempts to explain the Handy Cleaning Kit. He failed each time because he wasn't thoroughly familiar with the attachments.

The salesman just pointed to the instrument, trusting that the prospect could get worked up over it "long distance" instead of "telegraphically."

The salesman leaned on the counter, talking with the palm

of one hand.

The salesman had some peculiar habit, such as picking his teeth, or scratching his head.

The salesman tossed the illustrated booklet in front of the prospect, hoping she would open it up and see the things in the booklet that might interest her.

SUMMARY OF WHEELERPOINT 3

A good single sentence should reinforce "Tested Words" with "Tested Techniques."

The MOTION that accompanies utterance of words – the expression on your face at the time and the manner in which the "sales package" is handled – are a part *of* your successful sales presentation.

Say it quick – but *say it with gestures.*

Then, if possible, make the prospect imitate what you have done. Make *him a* part of your "show." It's the MONKEY-SEE, MONKEY-DO instinct in the buyer.

DEMONSTRATE – BUT DEMONSTRATE TO SELL!

If you want your selling words to "ring the bell" twice as hard, follow Wheelerpoint_3, and "SAY IT WITH FLOWERS" – and don't ask the prospect IF he wants to buy, but HOW and WHEN and WHERE and WHICH, the technique of closing a sale, which we will find in Wheelerpoint 4, in the next chapter.

Get action with action.

CHAPTER 4

DON'T ASK IF – <u>ASK WHICH!</u>

(Wheelerpoint 4)

By "Don't Ask If – Ask Which" I mean you should always frame your words (especially at the close) so that you give the prospect a choice between something and something, never between SOMETHING and NOTHING.

You will find a sale moving quicker to a successful close if you ask leading questions, as a good lawyer does, making it easy and natural for your prospect to say "Yes."

There are two kinds of salespeople, those who throw huge exclamation marks at you as they talk and those who hook your interest tactfully with question marks. Being a Question-Mark instead of an Exclamation-Mark salesman is the fourth difference between a winner and a loser in salesmanship.

THE VALUE OF THE WORD "WHICH"

The Exclamation-Mark salesman clubs his prospects with his pet ideas – and they flee out the nearest exit! He is always using such words as the following:

"I'm positive...!"
"I KNOW I'm right..."
"You MUST..."

He points his finger, he pounds the counter, he sticks out his chin, but he never asks the prospect a diplomatic question to find out if his sales talk is going over.

Hook the long curved arm of a question mark around your prospects and customers, and you will draw them nearer to the cash register or the dotted line – but be SURE you ask them questions that GET THE ANSWERS YOU WANT!

Never ask the prospect IF he wants to buy – but WHEN, WHAT, WHERE, and HOW! Not if – but which!

THESE QUESTIONS WON'T GET
THE REPLIES YOU WANT

"Could you afford the better-priced one?"

"Would you be interested in the dusting kit?"

"Would you like me to explain this feature to you?"

"Shall I demonstrate this to you?"

"How about it?"

"Howya fixed for a...?"

Don't be a "How-about-it?" salesman, or a "Howya-fixed-for-it?" salesman. These are bad expressions to acquire. *Eliminate them from your sales vocabulary.* They have grown "whiskers," and they lack "punch," as later chapters will show. They are not only "baggy in the knees" with a "shine in their seats," but they have grown "long beards." Avoid them!

BUT THESE QUESTIONS GET
THE ANSWERS YOU WANT

"You perhaps are wondering what Positive Agitation is,

aren't you?"

"You like this feature, don't you?"

"That's neat, isn't it?

"Which of these do you prefer?"

"When would you like delivery?"

"How do you prefer paying, weekly or monthly?"

"Where do you plan using it, here or over there?"

Ask the RIGHT question, especially in the close, and you'll get the answer *you* want – and the order will follow quickly.

TESTED QUESTIONS REVIVE
WAVERING SALES

Whenever you feel the sale wavering, ASK A TESTED QUESTION – one that will start you off on a new tack. A question gives you a breathing spell while the prospect is answering it. The question mark is also a good method of bringing objections into the open. The technique is very simple to acquire.

Whenever the prospect is wavering and tells you some reason for not buying, ASK HIM WHY. *"Why?" is the hardest one word for a prospect to answer!* He will struggle to answer your "why." He will find it difficult to put his objection into suitable words. His vague, distant, hidden objection is often so imaginary it CAN'T be framed in words. For instance, observe this example:

NELLIE: "I'll think it over."

SALESMAN: "Why?"

NELLIE: "Well – I – it just seems best."

15

By using this rule of "Why" you bring out all the objections of the prospect. Soon all the questions seem answered – but still the prospect won't buy. ONE KEY OBJECTION still worries the prospect. What is it? Cost? Weight? Construction? Practicality? Can't realize the need? Feels another has better features?

KEEP USING THE WORD "WHY"!

Ask him, *"Why* do you hesitate? – Why do you believe it is too costly? – Why do you want to wait until fall?" Keep him answering your "whys" until you find the REAL objection. Then when You ARE SURE you have discovered the real objection, handle it with this "tested technique":

SALESMAN: "Is that your ONLY REASON for not buying?"
NELLIE: "Yes, that's my only reason for not buying."

Nellie has committed herself! She is behind ONE objection! NOW ANSWER this key objection, and the sale will soon be yours!

When you do answer the objection, be sure to say: "You told me that was your ONLY REASON for not buying – so now I imagine you are ready to have me make delivery!"

SUMMARY OF WHEELERPOINT 4

Learn the legal knack of asking LEADING QUESTIONS, especially in the close, that get you the answers YOU want.

Never take a chance and ask a question unless you KNOW the reply it will get you.

Be a good lawyer – use leading questions and practice the rule of "Why."

Bring these "bogeymen" objections into the daylight with leading questions – and watch the bogeymen melt away like shadows!

Whenever you feel the sale wavering, practice Wheelerpoint 4, and ask a question – but don't ask IF – ask WHICH!

Ask WHEN and WHERE and HOW!

Then if you apply the fifth and final Wheelerpoint and watch HOW you say it as well as WHAT you say, as suggested on the next page, you will be master of most sales presentations that you make.

**You can catch more fish with hooks
than with crowbars.**

CHAPTER 5

WATCH YOUR BARK

(Wheelerpoint 5)

We come now to the last Wheelerpoint, and upon its proper execution hinges the test of how many of your sales words will succeed or fail – for your VOICE is the "carrier" of your message!

The finest "sizzle" that you telegraph in ten words in ten seconds, with a huge bouquet of "flowers" and lots of "Which," "When," "Where," and "How," FLOPS if the voice is FLAT.

It is not necessary or advisable to be an actor and elocute – but a PROPER TONE OF VOICE carries the message swifter and TRUER to the other person with least "static."

"HIS MASTER'S VOICE"

Consider how much the little dog can express with just one word and one tail to wag! What he can do with the tone of his "woof" and the wag of his tail in conveying his many messages is well worth emulating!

Watch the "bark" that can creep into your voice! Watch the "wag" behind your words!

DON'T BE A "JOHNNY-ONE-NOTE"

Train your voice to run its entire scale of tones. Read a

18

book out loud to yourself at night. Cup your hands behind your ears and hear yourself talk. This is excellent drilling in how to pitch your voice properly. Avoid a mechanical, monotonous voice. Inflect! Emphasize! Lower – raise – talk slow – then speed up dramatically. Vary the tempo of your words! *This makes you interesting to the listener.*

Don't be a Johnny-one-note. Learn to highlight your sales points by playing the full "organ" of your vocal chords – the entire range! Not just one note!

Be the director who can go from instrument to instrument.

Above all, avoid tone and voice peculiarities that attract attention to *themselves – rather than to your message.* Here are a few examples to illustrate this point:

SMILE WHEN YOU SAY THESE –
AND REACH FOR THE "DOTTED LINE"

"This will shorten your cleaning time by hours."

"You have only one back – one life to live."

"If men did the cleaning, we couldn't make these cleaners fast enough."

WHEN NELLIE SAYS, "I'LL THINK IT OVER,"
WAG THESE WORDS AT HER

"Think also of the DIRT that is ruining your rugs."

"Think of the MANY BACKACHES still in store for you."

WHEN NELLIE SAYS, "I'LL BUY LATER," TELE-
GRAPH THESE MESSAGES

"Would you continue to use a toaster that didn't work?"

"Would you use a washing machine that left clothes dirty?"

"What will you SAVE yourself by buying later – not your rugs or back – just two dimes a day!"

SUMMARY OF WHEELERPOINT 5

Have the "voice with the smile" – but the smile that is not insincere and automatically "turned on" for the immediate benefit of the prospect.

Don't ever smile insincerely, like the wolf at Red Riding Hood's door!

If you fail to smile, if you stick your chin out, or if you look grim, down and out, tired, bewildered, scared, or too confident, you are SIGNALING the prospect to BEWARE!

The last principle, therefore, to make your sales talk "stick" is to watch HOW you say it. So apply Wheelerpoint 5, "Watch Your Bark," and then watch your sale go down the road to SUCCESS!

The wooden Indian never made a sale.

THREE
OTHER
WHEELER
PRINCIPLES

1.   **The Law of Averages**

2.   **The X, Y, Z Formula**

3.   **The A and B Rule.**

CHAPTER 6

THREE LITTLE WORDS THAT SOLD MILLIONS OF SQUARE CLOTHESPINS

(The Law of Averages)

> *"While individuals may be insoluble puzzles, in the aggregate they become mathematical certainties."*
>
> *– Sherlock Holmes.*

This statement means that you can never foretell how any one person will react to a given selling sentence, but that you can say with scientific accuracy what the average will do. This philosophy of Sherlock Holmes is the best defense I know for the underlying philosophy of this book: that single sentences can be so constructed as to make *a majority of people buy.*

Several years ago manufacturers began to distribute square clothespins, instead of their famous round ones. Like most people I became curious and went into the first small store I came upon and asked the clerk what the *difference* was between the square and the round clothespins.

"Three cents a dozen *difference!*" said the salesgirl, snapping her gum in my face.

I asked the buyer in the little store and his answer was no better:

"I sell so many gross of clothespins a week, and this time

they happened to come in square – why, I don't know! But I do know I'll get *stuck* with them – for what woman will spend 3¢ extra a dozen for square ones!"

MANY REASONS FOR BEING SQUARE

I went to the home office of this chain of small stores, and I was told by the merchandising division that these are the "sizzles" in a square clothespin:

1. They won't slip out of wet hands so easily.
2. You can hold more in your wet hands.
3. They are polished and won't tear delicate garments.
4. They won't split on clotheslines.
5. They have knobs on the end so women can hold them in their mouths, especially if they don't have teeth.

Everything about these square clothespins was scientific – except what the salesperson said to the customers. While I was hearing these "sizzles," I accidentally dropped a clothespin on the floor, and a thought came to mind. I visualized a woman hanging up clothes. She has an armful of wash, clothespins in her wet hands and in her mouth as she starts across the kitchen floor. Suddenly a clothespin falls to the floor. Being round, it rolls under the stove. Like little dogs, clothespins love nothing better than to get under a stove and just lie there.

It may roll elsewhere. The woman fails to see it, and a few moments later she backs into it. Down goes the wash and the woman – and in comes the insurance adjuster!

Perhaps women would buy the square clothespins, I thought, if we told them this simple "sizzle": A square clothespin won't roll when it hits the floor; if a woman drops one, she has only to bend down, pick it up, and go on with her work. She would know at all times where the square clothespins were and would not trip up on them.

THE IDEA "CLICKS" WITH WOMEN

Taking this idea into our laboratory for polishing and smoothing, and then for tests behind the counters, we packed this selling point into a two-second "Tested Selling Sentence," and instructed salespeople to say, when women wanted to know *why* they were square:

"They won't roll!"

Three little words – yet they struck home across the busy counters, and customers began to buy them, showing again that what sells one woman often sells others!

STORY OF INDIAN MOCCASINS

Some time ago I was called into the Schulte-United Retail Stores to help devise selling language and techniques to sell Indian moccasins to small boys as an extra suggested sale to regular purchases.

Here is a composite sales talk used by the clerks in selling these moccasins to boys shopping with their mothers, with the "sizzle" buried in a long line of sales conversation. Can you pick it out?

SALESPERSON: "Madam, wouldn't you like to buy a pair of real Indian moccasins for your little boy here? They have triple stitching on the back and can't rip. The beads are put on with wire and will never break off. They have blunt toes instead of pointed ones; we call them our health moccasins, because your little boy's foot will grow straight and healthy all the rest of his life."

CUSTOMER: (Usual reply.) "Nope – just give me my package."

But when the salesperson was instructed to take the Indian moccasins and place them in *front of the little boy,* saying, "The kind the REAL INDIANS WEAR, Sonny!," sales increased!

That single sentence made the little boy's eyes pop out. He became an assistant salesman and would start selling his mother on why he should have a pair. Did he care if the moccasins were healthy or unhealthy? No! Did he care if the beads would last five minutes or five years? No – all he visualized was that he could wear them up and down the street and make his friends envious by saying:

"Whoopee! The kind the REAL INDIANS wear!"

We are all alike, and we all respond to the same "sizzles." This one sells three out of thirteen times it is used!

SELLING WHITE SHOE POLISH

Every one of you at some time or other has gone into a store to purchase some white shoe polish. You have heard many such selling statements as:

1. "It is liquid and spreads on easier."
2. "It won't rub off."
3. "It is in cake form and lasts longer."

4. "It keeps shoes white longer."

5. "Was 25¢ – now 15¢."

Which of these statements would influence you? Which do you think increased sales three hundred percent? Yes, you guessed it! Sentence 2.

The Hecht Company in Washington, D.C., had the three hundred percent sales increase, and today several manufacturers are using these four words as their main headline in advertisements and on billboards. All people want the white to stay on. It is a basic appeal!

THE STORY OF BARBASOL

I was asked by the Barbasol Company, in the person of F. B. Shields, president, to find a good "Tested Selling Approach" to use on men shopping in drugstores and at toilet goods counters.

Going to Sears, Roebuck & Company in Cleveland to set up our field word laboratory, we soon discovered there were 146 statements that could be used in approaching a customer, yet one came to the surface as best. It was:

"How would you like to save six minutes shaving?"

This is a surefire leading question, for what man could reply, "Not interested – I love to hang around the bathroom shaving!"

When the man asked *how* he could cut his shaving time, he was told:

"Use Barbasol – just spread it on – shave it off – nothing else required!"

Sales in this Sears store increased one hundred and two percent, with only one negative reaction. A man with fuzz on his face said, "My gracious, it only takes me three minutes to shave anyway!"

This answer gave us an idea, and the single-sentence sales "opener" was changed to, "How would you like to cut your shaving time *in half?*" When this even more basic approach was used at William Taylor's store in Cleveland, sales increased three hundred percent, according to reports from Richard Roth, vice president.

And here is further proof that once a sentence or sales appeal is basic, it will sell as high as seven out of every ten people on which it is used properly. The same sentence was sent to Benson, Smith & Company Honolulu, and in three days sold fifty-one out of seventy-eight people, *or the entire product on hand!*

Thousands of such case histories are in our files, but these are sufficient to indicate there is something fundamental about Sherlock Holmes' law of averages:

We are all alike and respond to the same buying urges, and the same emotions that sold customers 20,000 years ago sell them today.

Now let us see in the next chapter what these basic buying urges are so that we can direct our "Tested Selling Sentences" at them and thus eliminate "blind selling."

CHAPTER 7

TWO LITTLE WORDS THAT TURNED
NICKELS INTO DIMES

(The Wheeler X, Y, Z Formula)

> *Self-preservation is nature's oldest law, but the
> desire for romance and the desire for money are
> close behind it. The money appeal means, of course,
> that you can have what you want when you want it.
> This is the Wheeler "X, Y, Z" Formula that will teach
> you at what three basic buying urges to shoot your
> "sizzles."*

I am thirsty and stop at the first drugstore I come to. I step
up to the busy counter, motivated for a drink by the law of
self-preservation, for my throat is parched. I ask the clerk
for a Coca Cola, and he says, "Large or *small, sir?*"

The store loses a nickel. I am deprived of a longer moment
of refreshment, for like most people I automatically say,
"Small."

A thought occurred to me: Suppose the clerk had just said,
"Large one?"; would I have *automatically* told him, "Yes"?

I approached Mr. Harry Brown, store manager of Abraham
& Straus of Brooklyn, which has more fountain space under
one roof than any other store; and Fred Griffiths, president of
the Pennsylvania Drug Stores in New York. The experiment
was tried out. Whenever a customer asked for a Coca Cola, the

clerk would say, "Large one?" Five thousand tests were made, and results on our Copyrighted "Yes" and "No" Recording System showed that seven out of every ten people replied, "Yes!" This meant that out of every ten customers the stores received *35¢ extra* business and had more satisfied customers driven to quench their thirst by the law of self-preservation!

Two little words that turned nickels into dimes!

WHEELER "X, Y, Z" FORMULA

It doesn't take much persuasion to sell a person when you direct your "Tested Selling Sentences" at their basic buying motives, which are, in their order of importance:

1. *Basic buying motive of self-preservation.* First we must have food, clothing, and shelter for OURSELVES before we can think of others, even our mates. It is our oldest INSTINCT to look out for ourselves first, and so it is our oldest buying urge. *"X" symbolizes the basic buying motive of self-preservation.*

2. *Basic buying motive of romance.* Once we have food, clothing, and shelter, our thoughts turn to leisure, and so comes romance, another *natural* force in us. Desire for romance is not only for sex, but also for adventure, travel, and so on. It is our second strong instinct and our second basic buying motive. *"Y" symbolizes the basic buying urge of romance.*

3. *Basic buying motive of money.* With money we know we can purchase security; it gives us the knowledge that we can have food, clothing, shelter, and romance at will, whenever we so desire. Money being our third strongest instinct, it is our third biggest buying motive. *"Z" is the symbol of the money buying motive.*

There are, of course, many other buying motives, as any copywriter or sales manager will tell you – but the 105,000 selling statements in our library indicate that you can sell 85 percent of your prospects with just these three simple buying motives – *because they are so basic!*

Memorize this X, Y, Z Formula. You will find its simplicity an important part of its effectiveness. Don't complicate selling too much with too many rules or principles.

THE PROSPECT'S "MENTAL POCKETBOOKS"

Inside the prospect's brain are these three basic buying motives – three "mental pocketbooks." You must unlock them *first* before the brain will tell the prospect's hand to reach down into his pants pocket and get the *physical* purse.

What is most important to remember is that these three "mental pocketbooks" are not in the logical front part of the prospect's mind but are buried deep in the emotional *back* part of the brain. You must fashion your words so that they will fly past the prospect's cold reasoning, his logical front mind, and move, *emotionally,* his real basic buying urges in the "depth" of his brain.

THE "DESIRE" AND "FEAR" SELLING "SIZZLES"

Two strong forces that motivate the three "mental pocketbooks" in the prospect's mind are (1) fear and (2) desire. If we fear for our health, we are prompted to respond to medical advertisements addressed to our pet worry; and we respond to statements in advertisements about Florida or California, where health is supposed to be available under every palm tree (X).

If we desire to end money worries and become financially secure, we find ourselves listening to insurance men, bankers, or gold-brick sellers, provided they play upon our desire for money (Z).

If we bought from the logical front part of our minds, we would quickly out-reason the gold-brick seller, or the man with Brooklyn Bridge to turn over to us, or the old medicine man, or the circus barker.

Since we buy not from cold logic but from emotional urges, we respond to all forms of statements designed to motivate our three basic buying motives, and we are quick to reach for our cash when we read or hear:

"Corn gone in five days or your money back." (X)
"How to be the life of the party." (Y)
"End money worries quickly." (Z)
"Free roller skates." (Y)
"No down payment necessary." (Z)
"Be an executive while still young." (X, Y, Z)
"Removes every trace of dandruff." (X, Y)

We won't admit that we buy emotionally – but we do! That fact must never be lost sight of, nor the fact that the same emotional urges that made Caesar buy, if basic, will make your next customer buy!

SELLING BUTTONLESS UNION SUITS

The greatest desire of every mother is to be relieved from some of her daily tasks, such as dressing and undressing little Willy five times a day (X). Realizing this, I had a young lady in Saks 34th Street one day, at the suggestion of H. L. Redman, president, experiment with selling sentences to promote the sale of a new buttonless union suit. Of over thirty different selling "sizzles" in the garment, the one that sold the garments, which cost 25¢ more than those with buttons, was:

"The little boy can put it on ALL BY HIMSELF!"

That single sentence gave the mother a desire she had always dreamed about, and it is basic enough to sell the suits to any mother with the 25¢ extra to spend.

SELLING EXPENSIVE SAFETY PINS

The fear of every mother – and of women who are not mothers – is to have a safety pin burst open at the wrong moment and stab the wearer (X). Therefore, Saks' clerks sold handfuls of safety pins that cost five cents more per package than most on the market, by this single sentence:

"They won't burst open in the garment and cause injury!"

Another worry – and also a desire of mothers – is to have diapers that won't chafe or cause injury to their children (X), and when the form–fitting diapers came out, they sold when the Saks' clerks used this "Tested Selling Sentence":

"They are form-fitting, and require only ONE safety pin!"

SELLING SHADOW-PROOF SLIPS

A desire and a need of women, especially in the South where there is plenty of sunlight and wide streets, is for a slip that is constructed in such a manner that it is concealing even in strongest sun glare (X). This problem was solved by several manufacturers long before the clerks began to dramatize this "sizzle" to the women rather than consume time talking about the fine needlework.

When the Hecht Company got behind the idea, and every sale was started with this single sentence, sales of the slips increased sixty percent, according to the case record in our files. The sentence was this:

"It is shadow-proof – even on sunniest days!"

This is another example of self-preservation, the X portion of the Wheeler formula.

ROMANCE ("Y") SELLS FURNITURE

After every regular sale in the Hecht Company, I had the salespeople one summer take the women shoppers to a comfortable lounging chair and say:

"This is our new napping chair."

When the women inquired what a "napping chair" was, the salespeople would say:

"It is scientifically constructed to allow the head to rest comfortably, making napping a real pleasure (Y). Try it."

Mr. Charles Dulcan, vice president, stated that sales increased about ten percent in this item during this single sentence "drive."

COCKTAIL LAWN SWINGS ARE SOLD

One time when Mr. James Rotto, former sales promotion manager of the Hecht Company, noticed lawn swings not selling very well, he called us in from our branch word laboratory constructed in the store, and set us to work digging up "sizzles."

After a little research, it was discovered that these lawn swings had an arm that would hold cocktail glasses without spilling the contents, or causing them to fall off and break. When this ONE "sizzle" was called to the attention of customers, they lost interest in the less expensive and advertised swings, and started to buy these. This is one "sizzle" that brought salespeople $5.00 more per customer and brought added enjoyment to customers.

The romantic urge of a cocktail! (Y)

The desire to have a drink convenient, the fear of breaking a glass, a basic selling sentence that works! Try it sometime!

SELLING ELECTRIC LIGHT BULBS

Completing some of the other outstanding examples at the Hecht Company, let me sum up how seven hundred extra electric light bulbs were sold one July by the simple sentence:

"It will make the new shade even prettier!" (Y)

And twenty out of a hundred people shopping in Sears, Roebuck in Cleveland, according to Jack North of the Electrical League, bought when this simple sentence was used as an opening wedge:

"Are you in the kitchen much, Madam?"

When the customer asked why, the salesperson advised a 100 or 150 watt lamp because, "You can read the smallest print in a cookbook." (X)

The mousetrap will ALWAYS spring at the psychological moment, if you bait it with the right "sizzles" – those that fly by the cold logic of the customer and move him emotionally!

When the Paris Garter people wanted to sell suspenders, they created one that would not slide off the shoulder. According to Joseph M. Kraus, they used the single sentence, "They won't SLIDE OFF the shoulders (X)," and went from eighteenth place in the industry up to third!

Don't forget these three basic buying motives: self-preservation (X), romance (Y), and money (Z). They'll make money for you, if you let them. Remember that the HEART is closer to the customer's pocketbook than his BRAIN!

CHAPTER 8

THEY SOLD BROOKLYN BRIDGE
AGAIN LAST WEEK

(The Wheeler *A* and *B* Rule)

> *"A" is the statement of fact; "B" is the proof. Confidence men sold gold bricks because proof was never required in the old days. Today it is. People now want to hear – feel – see – and hold what they are about to purchase.*

I read in the newspapers a few weeks ago that someone was again arrested for selling Brooklyn Bridge, and often I hear about somebody who bought a gold brick, even in this day of the F. B. I., the G-men, and the radio.

The reason is that there are still a few people who don't require proof, but they are few in number. The young lady in the W. T. Grant store who sold square clothespins by saying, "They won't roll," would "Say it with flowers" *and drop one on the counter to prove her point.*

The Pocahontas Oil salesman who used our "Tested Selling Sentences" to inform motorists their new windshield wipers "had triple blades, and cleaned three times as fast," handed a blade through the open window to the motorist to *see, feel,* and *inspect!*

A RULE TO REMEMBER IN WORD FORMATION

When Uncle Jake listened at the corner store to the man in the derby with the option on Brooklyn Bridge and heard that he could charge a toll rate of ten cents per person and make a million, he wanted to buy the bridge. Uncle Jake didn't question the transaction because the salesman "looked honest and had a nice flow of talk." So Uncle Jake mortgaged his home and bought Brooklyn Bridge for $565.00 in cash!

Today, however, Uncle Jake wants proof. He likes to hear statements of fact (A), but he wants proof as well (B). The rule to remember, therefore, to convince more people faster is to tell them the benefits and advantages they will receive from what you are selling, and then *prove them* in some way. This is the Rule of *A* and *B* – *A* standing for the benefit and *B* for the PROOF.

"I WEAR 'EM MYSELF" PROVES NOTHING TODAY

Salespeople used to say, "I wear 'em myself," and customers would buy, but that statement is too overworked now. Besides, the customer today doesn't want to feel that the salesperson, of all people, will wear or own the same thing he will purchase.

The fact that "Mrs. Jones has one" is only of mild importance these days, according to our research behind the counters of such important stores as R. H. Macy & Company, B. Altman, and the May Company stores, although the "testimonial" is still effective if handled delicately. "It's our biggest seller," sometimes proves effective, because you do not pin it down on any one person; but it is rather trite.

When the street hawker claims, "These combs won't break, chip, or crack," he will slam a comb forcefully in front of him, and run a large file over the surface, dramatically "Saying it with flowers" – instinctively applying the *B* portion of the *A* and *B* Rule.

Tell the benefits (A), then give them proof (B), if you want sales to move faster!

"FEEL" – "SEE" – "HOLD"

These are three words that you should have in your everyday vocabulary for ready use in convincing people on the spot for a quick sixty-second close. Get customers to feel the sales package; get them to hold it! Say, "FEEL the fine texture of these stockings!" Or, "Just HOLD this handle and SEE how it fits your grip!"

The refrigerator man says, "Try this yourself. See how easily it opens!"

The Johns-Manville man tells his prospect that their Rock Wool will keep heat inside the house, and to prove this point he takes the family out into the street. He points to the roof of the house down the street which has Rock Wool Insulation and says, "See the snow on Mr. Brown's roof? That's a sign heat doesn't go through his roof and melt the snow. The snow on your roof, however, has melted because you don't have insulation."

This is convincing language to the prospect, and the J. M. salesman closes by saying, "You are trying to heat the outdoors. Your coal bills must be high, aren't they? Why the cost of Rock Wool in your home will pay for itself within three years!"

It isn't HOW MUCH IT COSTS, but HOW MUCH IT SAVES, that counts!

"THE BUTTONS ARE ANCHORED ON THE SHIRTS"

The May Company, of Baltimore, took our "Tested Selling Sentence" for men's shirts, "The buttons are anchored on and won't break off in the wringer," and gave it to their salespeople. Sales were fair; but when the clerks began "saying it with flowers" and started to tug on the buttons, dramatically, in front of the customers, sales tripled!

Customers heard the "owner benefit" (A), and then saw proof of it (B); and because of the "monkey-see, monkey-do instinct" in all of us, they would take the shirts into their OWN HANDS and tug on the buttons to convince themselves!

THEY DON'T ALWAYS WORK, THOUGH

I have often been asked, "Do you have trouble in finding selling sentences?" Of course we do. Hundreds of times. Often many tests are made before a single word is discovered.

For instance, we had the idea that we could sell Macy's Men's Featherweight Shirts by placing them on the counter, having the clerk say, "See how light they are!" and then blow them off the counter into the customer's hands.

Fine drama! Ten-second words that conveyed the sale's idea! But the idea failed! The first Macy clerk didn't have enough "lung power" to raise the shirt off the counter; one ex-football player blew it over the customer's shoulder; and two other salesmen had breaths filled with cigarette smoke that almost "gassed" their customers. Here was a fine idea that

39

failed the first ten minutes it was tested.

Then we created this idea. The clerk would take a broad-cloth shirt, place it into the right hand of the customer and say, "Feel the weight of this shirt." The clerk would then take the broadcloth and hand the customer the lighter Featherweight, saying, "Now feel the weight of THIS shirt!" The great difference in weight was felt by the customer at once!

A nice example of the principles of selling in ten seconds, with plenty of owner benefits *(A)* and proof *(B)!*

PICTURES GIVE PLENTY OF PROOF

L. D. Cassidy, of the Johns-Manville Company, has shown me pictures of kitchens before and after being remodeled, as proof that their products do transform ugly kitchens into dream kitchens.

The Johns-Manville man opens many a sale with this "Tested Selling Sentence": "How would you like to see the kitchen we have just done over for Mrs. Smith down the street?"

This leading question gets him the answer he wants.

Remember the Rule of *A* and *B.* Shoot out your benefits first – but prove them the next second. When you send a post-card and say, "Having a good time…," you pick out the best-looking scene to prove the point!

The proof of the pudding is in the eating, and if you want to step up your selling ability 25%, start qualifying your statements with proof, by learning the many ways to "Say it with flowers."

PERTINENT EXAMPLES OF WHEELERPOINTS, RULES, PRINCIPLES AND FORMULAS

CHAPTER 9

YOUR FIRST TEN WORDS ARE MORE IMPORT-
ANT THAN THE NEXT TEN THOUSAND

*You have only ten short seconds to capture the fleet-
ing attention of the other person, and if in those ten
short seconds you don't say something mighty
important, he will leave you – either physically or
mentally!*

Everywhere you go you read a sign that says, "Don't
write – TELEGRAPH!" There is a definite reason for
this slogan, and for choosing it as our second Wheelerpoint. No matter how busy a man is, when a telegram arrives
it gets his immediate attention. The sender was forced to boil
into ten words the entire "sizzle" of his message – so his story
was told in ten seconds, and naturally "rang the bell."

Little Willy wants an extra slice of bread and jam; Big
Brother wants the car for the evening; Dad wants to go out and
play cards with the boys; and Mother wants a new hat. Uncle
Joe is planning a sales program for a new cosmetic; Sister Sue
wants her beau to take her to Bermuda on their honeymoon;
and around the corner the preacher is planning a visit on the
household to make it church-conscious. *Their first ten words
will be more important than their next ten thousand!*

THE RIGHT COMBINATION

Everybody in the office knows the numerals on the dial of the safe, yet only a few know the COMBINATION of those numbers that will unlock the safe and reveal the riches that lie therein.

So it is with selling. Every salesman knows the many "sizzles" of his product – he knows the numerals inside his sales kit, but what he often doesn't know is the RIGHT COMBINATION of those selling words to make people buy. One thing is certain – he must boil his "sizzles" down to the fewest possible and his sales talk to the least number of words to get the big message across to the other person.

This we learned in the chapters on the five Wheelerpoints, but for a moment now let us see the psychological reasons that underlie these Wheelerpoints. It is interesting to know WHY something happens as well as to know that it happens.

WHY YOU MUST GET TEN-SECOND ATTENTION

As you walk to work your mind is fleeting from thought to thought and your eye from object to object – you are doing what is known as "daydreaming." You see everything – yet *see nothing!* Your mind is miles away. You are building castles in Spain. Automatically you tip your hat, automatically you dodge a street car, and instinctively you walk around people who may bump into you. You are awake – yet *sound asleep!* You are in a daze.

Then somebody uses a "Tested Selling Sentence" on you. It penetrates the "cloud." You come to life – down to earth! You are all eyes and ears. The "sizzle" captured your attention.

We must learn the secret of getting our words INTO the other person's brain – by the haze and past the daze – for the prospect may be "Looking at us, eye to eye, *yet his mind may be miles away.*" As Richard Borden says, "You must have an 'Oh hum crasher' for your prospect!" You must crash his "Oh hum" – his yawn – you must use words that dash by his daze.

"Stop, look, and listen" means nothing today to people; they look at it, yet every day people are being hit by trains. It is not a good split-second "daze crasher" anymore because we have seen it too often.

Go over your vocabulary. How many "daze crashers" have you, along with "door crashers" and "telephone crashers"? Pretty few, I'll bet, if you are like the average salesman. Better stock up on some. They will come in handy to penetrate the other person's "castles in Spain" – to change that glassy, far away look into one of keen attention!

This is why our first Wheelerpoint is, "Don't sell the steak – sell the sizzle," and our second one is, "Don't write – TELE-GRAPH." This is why we advise you to "watch your first ten seconds – your first ten words!"

WHEN YOU GET TEN-SECOND ATTENTION – THEN WHAT?

Once you have been successful in crashing the prospect's "Oh hum" or his daze with a "sizzle," then you have about three short minutes to get your message into his mind – his blood – his system. You have three short minutes before his mind will wander away, saturated!

After walking five miles, after reading several chapters, or

44

after talking for some time, our muscles, our mind, and our spirit wilt and grow weary and fatigued because we have saturated ourselves. A blotter holds just so much ink, and then it becomes "fatigued"; it is saturated, and it is useless to the writer.

Our case histories indicate that Mr. Prospect fatigues when you talk for more than three minutes without letting him talk, without using some showmanship to renew his interest, or without changing the topic. He can concentrate just three minutes; then he wants to talk; he wants to try it; he wants to participate. For this reason we have developed Wheelerpoint 3, "Say it with flowers," which teaches you to make the prospect *a part* of your sales show.

OUR LIE DETECTOR TESTS

A number of years ago I experimented at Johns Hopkins University with a lie detector, to see if certain "sizzles" would make people respond quicker than others, and we received definite proof that they would. We adjusted the little quartz string to a "customer," and recited a long sales talk to him or her, and on going over the film afterwards noted wherein we had received mental reactions.

These findings indicated a three-minute fatigue point, beyond which the sales talk fails to register efficiently. They also indicated that words affect people *physically* as well as mentally, and so we offer you our Fourth Wheelerpoint, "Don't ask if – ask which," to help you close sales quickly, before saturation sets in!

Take the word *lemon.* Visualize biting into a nice juicy lemon, and note how your salivary glands will function. Speak the word to somebody, and talk about cutting the lemon. *Watch his mouth water.*

If you want to dry his mouth, ask him to visualize a mouthful of hot, dry cotton. This thought will tend to dry the salivary glands, just as the thought of the word *alum* tends to pucker the lips of those who hear it.

Then I was sales adviser to Dave Rubinoff, showman violinist, he informed me how he could move people physically, as well as mentally, with his musical "sales notes." If he played "Humoresque" soft and low, the ducts in the eyes would water up; the "St. Louis Blues" caused spines to wiggle; "Lover, Come Back to Me" prompted the ladies' hearts to beat faster; and a Sousa's march always made the feet of the men beat in time.

Such is the EMOTIONAL POWER of word tones on the human system! This accounts for Wheelerpoint 5, "Watch your bark," because your voice is the carrier of your "tested words."

A GOOD SALES EXAMPLE OF THESE FACTS

As a good example of the fact you have ten seconds to get attention and must tell your story in three minutes before saturation takes place, note this sales talk of L. D. Caulk Company, makers of silver alloy for the teeth. This sales talk, which I developed with William Grier, president of the company, was designed to be used on dentists, who have only a very few minutes to give to any dental salesman. They are professional men, and their time is valuable. Realizing this, we took the Five Wheelerpoints, and built this three-minute talk:

SALESMAN: (Daze crasher) "How would you like to INSURE your restorations for one cent per filling, doctor?"

DENTIST: (Looks up from work, curious) "How?"

SALESMAN: "The Chinaman charges you one cent for insuring your shirts, and by using Twentieth Century Alloy you can insure *your* reputation for one cent per filling. (Dentist becomes interested.)

"Run-of-the-mill alloy, you see, doctor, costs you about three cents per filling, and our T. C. alloy costs only four cents – but this is what you get for that extra cent: (Dentist now keenly interested.)

"First, you get scientifically graded alloy that is *easy to carve,* and that will adapt itself to the sides of the patient's tooth and *prevent seepage* and *thermal shocks.*

"Second, our T. C. alloy has particles with 'silver overcoats,' and because each particle contains *more silver,* the biting edge of the patient's filling will be stronger." Third, these 'silver overcoats' keep the filling silver bright *forever in the patient's mouth!*

"Those three important things are worth one cent more per filling, aren't they, doctor?"

MAKE EVERY SALE WITHIN SATURATION POINT

Summed up, if you want to make your sales more accurate, more foolproof, and faster, you must, for *biological* as well as for psychological reasons, follow the five Wheelerpoints, which teach:

You have only ten short seconds to penetrate the "day-dreaming" of the other person, and you must concentrate your best "sizzles" into three minutes, so the prospect will not YAWN, physically or mentally!

Each Wheelerpoint is based on this philosophy, which underlies all successful "Tested Selling Sentences." First you get the "sizzles," and then you express them "telegraphically," "saying it with flowers" to dramatize and prove your points; and by asking WHICH, not if, you bring your close *within* the fatigue point.

The tone of your voice as you are performing these simple points is important, for the best message will fall flat if the telegraph operator fails to click his keys properly!

Make your prospects' mouths water for MORE by never saturating or fatiguing them, for anyone becomes bored when he cannot take part in the game, and every actor knows that the time to stop is WHEN THEY WANT MORE! Even the circus parade soon wearies the eye when we watch too long, and the third chocolate soda begins to taste bitter!

Therefore, RIGHT NOW, go back over the five Wheeler-points. Memorize them! Interpret them into your OWN business! Find the "sizzles" in what you are selling, and practice putting these "sizzles" into ten-second "telegrams." Ask yourself how you can say your "sizzles" with "flowers." Can you bring about swifter closes, using the technique of the good lawyer, with his "Which," "Where," "When," and "How"? Then study your voice delivery. Does it sound convincing, honest, sincere?

If you can answer these questions with a "Yes," then you are doing about all that any salesman can to create interest, desire, and eventual purchase of whatever you are selling!

The principle is simple:

Parade your selling "sizzles" in telegraphic language with "flowers" so that no sales sequence is longer than three minutes at a stretch!

CHAPTER 10

THE FARMER'S DAUGHTER
MOVES TO TOWN

Don't try to hoodwink her today. She knows more about Broadway than the traveling salesman does. Hokum is gone with the wind. People are fountain-pen shy and sales-talk conscious.

M r. Charles Lesser, president of Bost Toothpaste Company, invited our Institute to study what should be said and done to sell his toothpaste in drug stores. After making a survey in a series of drug stores, we arrived at a method tested to sell the product at the cigar counters of the drug stores.

Again the "how about it–?" salesman was discarded, and the modern question-mark salesman was substituted. After a customer purchased some tobacco, the clerk would say

"Have you ever used the *smoker's tooth paste?*"

It was natural for the customer to say that he was not famil-iar with such a paste, and with this opportunity, with complete attention secured, the clerk would hold up a tube of Bost Toothpaste and say:

"It is made ESPECIALLY for people who smoke."

Here was a unique sort of toothpaste. The benefit was obvious. If the customer demanded proof, the salesman would blow cigarette smoke through his handkerchief, and rub away the stain with a little of the paste. (Wheelerpoint 3, "Say it with flowers.")

Results: The Standard Drug Stores of Ohio sold a three months' supply of Bost Toothpaste in one week, according to one record in our file on this "Tested Selling Sentence."

THE BARN HAS A DOUBLE LOCK

A few years ago J. C. Penney Company, operating 1,400 stores nationally, felt that if their salespeople would say the right thing at the right time, they would sell better quality merchandise and more of it to every customer.

I was given the assignment by Mr. W. A. Reynolds, vice president, of developing a word laboratory for these great stores, to analyze the selling features and owner benefits of each piece of merchandise. In particular, I recall an incident that increased the sales of a high-quality pair of bloomers. When women asked for "something in bloomers," the clerks would show two types at two different prices, and say of the better one, *"It has double-lock seams that won't split!"* Most Penney stores are in small towns, and sell to women who know something about the value of two locks on a barn door, and when they were told the seams had "double locks," those two words told them more than a thousand fancy words.

Picking the right words makes people respond and cash registers dance in musical glee!

SELLING PIE A LA MODE

It is the desire of every restaurant owner to sell his pie with a scoop of ice cream on top, for the pie tastes better, the eater is happier, and the restaurant has increased the average check by 10¢.

"Like a dab of ice cream?" will never induce people, for they carry that depression "no" on their tongues, and will say "no" first and think afterwards.

We were given this assignment by the Schulte-United stores for their restaurants. There were thirty-six possible methods of asking a customer if he would care for some ice cream on his pie.

Finally, we reverted to the old principle and had the waitresses ask, "Would you care for an order of *vanilla* or *chocolate* ice cream on your pie?" The mind of the customer would fluctuate between vanilla and chocolate, not between ice cream and no ice cream. Whichever he decided upon meant a happier customer – and a richer restaurant proprietor.

"Which" is a stronger word than "if." It is better to use a question mark to "hook" your proposition on to a prospect than an exclamation mark to "club" him into responding.

The hook is more potent than the crowbar!

THE EXCLAMATION SALESMAN IS GONE

Back in the days when the farmer's daughter lived on the farm, it was the custom to bewilder the prospect with a flow of "big-time talk" punctuated with exclamation marks. With one hand hooked in his vest, and his derby tilted back on his head, the drummer would dazzle the farmer's daughter with stories of the Gay White Way.

But the farmer's daughter has moved to town, mentally. There is no mystery anymore about the big city. She sees movies of the White Way. She reads magazines. She has a car that takes her to town. She knows more about New York and Hollywood than the traveling salesman does today.

So don't try the old hokum! People today are "sales-minded." They are "fountain-pen shy." They are conscious of selling tactics today, and they demand proof (B). They don't want to be sold; they want to buy.

WHEN YOU ARE "LOST FOR WORDS"

It is very effective to ask questions that *make misstatements* about something on which the other person is an expert. He immediately jumps up to correct you.

There are times, in this day and age when the farmer's daughter knows more about Fifth Avenue styles than many people living in the Bronx, when she becomes conscious that you are asking her questions to get her talking. To avoid this feeling on the part of the other fellow, make a *misstatement* sometime about golf, fishing, or some trade or hobby in which he prides himself on being an authority. Watch how quick he sits up and takes notice. Watch him begin "to set you right." It is good "Tested Technique." Try it sometime and test it out yourself.

THE STORY OF BUTTER

I. W. and George Bickley run Philadelphia's largest butter-and-egg house. On hearing our address before the Philadelphia Rotary and Poor Richard's Club, they invited me to make a study of how to build a modern sales presentation on butter and eggs.

Several talks were developed, and one for use on restaurant

owners was as follows:

"Mr. Jones, did you know that Bickley butter spreads MORE SLICES of bread per pound than most other brands?"

The restaurant owner was interested, of course, in learning how to reduce his butter cost, but being skeptical, would smile at the salesman and tell him it was impossible.

The salesman then said, "Have you ever spread butter on a slice of bread and had it stick in one corner, or spread thin and spotty over the bread?"

This is an experience of all of us, and so the restaurant man was forced to say he had often noticed this in his restaurant and that it was the reason why guests used so many pats of butter. When he demanded PROOF that Bickley butter would not stick in spots, it was given to him in a swift "Tested Selling" manner.

THE "YOUR OPINION" APPROACH

Another interesting question-mark approach devised for this butter-and-egg house is the "your opinion" approach. With the assistance of M. A. McCarron, sales manager, this approach was devised:

"I'm from the Bickley Company. I have been sent to get YOUR OPINION on how we can help grocers increase their butter and egg business!"

How much better this approach is than the usual, "Need any eggs today?" or "Howya fixed for butter, Mr. Jones?"

Ask people for their opinions. It is good philosophy; both of you will get along better and learn a lot more. Try it on your next customer – or the next friend you meet.

Another good rule to remember is:

When you are "lost for words" – ask questions!
But, make sure the questions are not obvious,
for the farmer's daughter has moved to town.

CHAPTER 11

THE BEST-LOOKING DOTTED LINE
WON'T SIGN ITSELF

> *When the time comes for you to get action, do so in sixty seconds, before "sales-talk fatigue" sets in on him. The proof of the pudding is the dotted line! Watch for the "brass ring."*

Like the merry-go-round that gives you a chance on every complete circle to catch the brass ring, every sales cycle gives you many chances to get the prospect's signature.

Nell was the beauty of the village and had many promising sweethearts, but one day she married the least wealthy, the homely fellow with a heart of gold perhaps, but with none in his pocketbook. When she was asked why, with all her attractive charms, she chose the poorest boy of all her beaux, she said, very sweetly, "He was the only one who *asked me* to marry him!"

If you want a signature, ask for it!

THE TECHNIQUE OF GETTING SIGNATURES

The technique of getting signatures is not the sudden flash of an order pad or a gold-plated fountain pen. It is more subtle today.

The Johns-Manville man gets "tactful action" when he asks the wife and husband, "Where do you prefer the spare room, in the attic or in the cellar?" (Wheelerpoint 4.) If they agree (which is seldom), the salesman wins; if they argue where it should be, he still wins, for no matter WHERE it will be finally, or who wins out, he gets the order!

I have seen W. W. Powell, training director of the Hoover vacuum cleaner, bring on many a diplomatic close in this way:

"You perhaps wonder why we call this our 150 model?"

The prospect asks why, and Powell says

"Because you can own it for only one-fifty per week. – That's wonderful news, isn't it?"

If the woman informs him she doesn't buy without consulting her husband, he says:

"Why $1.50 per week is only about two dimes a day. You spend that much for knick-knacks, don't you?"

DON'T ASK FOR SIGNATURES –
BUT "APPROVALS"

So many people have "signed papers" and got into difficulties that the expression "Sign your name" is one to avoid.

How much better it is to say:

"Place your approval here, sir."
"This is the place for your OK."
"Just put your initials here."

Don't lunge for a fountain pen. You'll give your prospect a fright! Get the pen and order pad out EARLY in the sale, so that the prospect will be accustomed to seeing it. Get it into their hands, if possible. One Hoover man does it by putting dirt from the floor on the order pad and rubbing it with his pencil, saying:

"Hear the grit? It is ruining your rugs."

He puts the pad and pencil into the prospect's hands for her to "test" the dirt and hear the grit. The pad and pencil is "planted" early in the sale for the signature – for the time when the merry-go-round gets in line with the brass ring!

USE "WHEN," NOT "IF"

Never use the word "if" – say "when"! For instance:

WRONG: "If you decide to buy, I'm sure you'll enjoy it!"
RIGHT: *"When you buy it, you'll enjoy it!"*
WRONG: "If you will go for a demonstration ride …"
RIGHT: *"When you have a demonstration ride..."*

"If" is weak! Avoid it. It has "whiskers" on it! It weakens your argument. You admit there is a doubt when you use it. "When" is a strong, positive word. Cultivate it!

"If" is negative! "When" is optimistic!

HOWARD DUGAN GOES TO TOWN

Howard Dugan, former manager of the Cleveland Hotel Statler, now vice president of this hotel chain, profited by his "Tested Selling" work with us. It was up to him to renew interest in the Great Lakes Exposition for the second year and to get double the preceding year's financial support from Cleveland businessmen.

58

Howard Dugan did not call up the exposition's supporters and explain he had been assigned to get twice as much money from each as they had contributed the year before. Instead he charted a sales talk with a sixty-second ACTION in mind. When the brass ring came around, he wanted to be sure to GRAB it!

Here is his famous telephone sales talk that "clicked":

"Do you realize, Bill, that the Great Lakes Exposition committee is thinking about *tripling* your appropriation for next year?"

What a message to TELEGRAPH – but it got quick interest on the other end of the wire! With attention secured, Howard brought out his best "sizzle." He began selling the bubbles on the Erie Shore – not the debris. He said, "Now I have a plan. I believe you fellows should only *double* your last years' appropriation – not triple it!"

The man on the other end connived with Howard and agreed, so here was the brass ring, and Howard caught it fast, saying, "I'm glad you agree that double is enough! It will save all of us money. So send me your check *right now* by messenger. I'll take it over to the committee myself this afternoon – and tell them DOUBLE is enough, before they can hold a meeting and triple the amount!"

The checks poured in. An entire city was sold an idea. The Great Lakes Exposition went into its second year of success!

The rule to remember is this: The dotted line won't sign itself. You Must ASK the other person to sign up if you want his order. You will have an opportunity ever so often in the sale to GRAB THE BRASS RING. When you see it, catch it in sixty seconds, before it gets away from you – before the other person can think up objections!

59

And when you get the signature – run, don't walk, to the nearest exit!

WIN DECISIONS – NOT ARGUMENTS

Win decisions – not arguments. Never disagree with a customer who offers an objection. Tactfully inform him he is wrong. When you show the customer you welcome objections, you disarm him.

Never let the customer feel that you are irritated by questions and objections. Welcome them – with a confident smile. A woman may look at a vacuum cleaner and say, "Doesn't it use a lot of electricity?" Then you should say, "You might think so because the suction is so powerful; but, in fact, it uses little electricity." You have tactfully informed the customer the instrument did NOT use much current. If you had said, "Of course it doesn't use much electricity," you would have become tangled in an argument.

If the customer says, "It looks heavy to me," don't say, "Heavy? Of course not." Instead say, "It does LOOK heavy, but feel how light it is."

Seem to agree, but bring the prospect diplomatically around to your way of thinking.

DON'T "OVERANSWER" OBJECTIONS

Don't offer a long explanation in answer to an objection, as you will incite suspicion in the other person. Meet the objection swiftly *and with few words*. A brief answer gives the prospect less opportunity to "come back," less to hang an argument onto! The longer *you* talk, the more time the person has to think up new objections. Keep the other person talking, and you do the thinking. Get the person to talk by asking him questions about what you are selling, such as:

"Which do you prefer?"
"Do you like this color, or this?"
"Is this the size you need?"
"This is built solidly, isn't it?"
"This feels smooth, doesn't it?"

Keep the customer "yessing" you – not "noing" you. The know-it-all customers must be handled carefully. Agree with them, and say:

"Since you know so much about this, I am sure you will agree this is the best make, won't you?"

"You are a sensible buyer, and I know this will please you."

"This is the kind you seem to like."

Don't let the know-it-all get you into an argument. Win the decision – not the argument. Be a "Yes, *but–*' salesman. Say "Yes," and then bring up the "but."

Better still, capitalize on the know-it-all by saying, "I am always glad to find a person who really knows this subject. Now tell me, *which* of these two would you say was the most practical?"

RESPECT THE "KNOW-IT-ALL"

Let the know-it-all feel that you respect his or her opinions. Once you have this confidence, he will listen to you. He is easy to sell after this point.

Don't try to cut off the know-it-all, or the "fussy" customer, or the "particular" customer. Let them talk on. Let them *unwind* themselves.

Sometimes the know-it-all is the third party. Don't overlook or shun the third party. Draw him into the sale by such questions as these:

"What is YOUR opinion, sir?"
"Which do you prefer, madam?"
"What do you think?"

Never lose sight of the fact that you are out to win decisions, not arguments. Avoid arguments with the "Yes – but" technique. Say things that get a "Yes" from your customer.

**Remember the rule: Win the decisions
and not the arguments.**

CHAPTER 12

HOW TO TAKE THE "TEMPERATURE"
OF THE PROSPECT

> *We look on the wall to see the temperature of the room – to determine whether it is too hot or too cold – and just how to adjust the windows. We should learn to take the "temperature" of the prospect as well.*

After we talk a few moments with the prospective customer, it is up to us to take the "temperature" of the prospect to see if he is hot or cold to our proposition, to set a proper course for a close.

There are certain questions we can use on the other person to determine his "state of feelings," words that tell us a great deal when they are used to take his "temperature." Here are a few questions to use:

"Which do you prefer, this one or that one?"

"Do you think the cord is long enough?"

"That is easy to understand, isn't it?"

"Would you pay in cash, or by check?"

"How do you usually pay for these things?"

"Would you have it sent to your home?"

"Would you keep it in the living room?"

"Would you include your boy in this policy?"

These are statements that get the other person to start talking, and most of these questions are formed in such a manner that the other person can't say "No" or "Yes," but must do some talking.

By getting him to talk we "warm him up." Just as a cold motor must be warmed up, so must a cold prospect. The more he talks the more he tells us of his objections, desires, wishes, ambitions, likes, and dislikes. On these we can determine our procedure – on these we can build up the next step in our sales presentation.

Always be sure that you take the "temperature" of the customer several times during the sale, just as the physician does to guide him in his next steps.

Keep selling the "sizzle" – and keep "saying it with flowers," which is showmanship, performance, PROOF!

THE ART OF CLOSING

Be sure never to lose sight of the results, benefits, and advantages of YOUR merchandise, YOUR product, YOUR sales package!

The art of making quick closes is in having confidence that you have picked the right "sizzles" for the customer and in reflecting *your confidence* so as to inspire the other person. Say:

"I feel sure this will fit your particular need."

"This is the best type for your purpose."

"This will work better for your specific requirement."

"I am sure this is just the right one for you."

"You will find this most convenient for your purpose."

"You will enjoy this one very much, I know."

Don't show doubt by saying such things as, "It seems what you need," or "Perhaps this will do," "Maybe–." Be specific! Direct! Positive! Confident!

Often the other person indicates when you take his "temperature" that he wants to hear more, or "see others," or "get a lower price." If the prospect is sincere, he will use such language as:

"I don't like this particular style."
"That isn't quite what I want."
"Haven't you something a little smaller?"
"Isn't there something at a lower price?"
"What other colors does this come in?"

When you hear these "sincere" remarks, show more, give more information, or quote other prices – or compromise in some way. The person wants to buy, but is not "sold" on the particular things you have offered up to that moment.

Here are a few statements used by timid people and hesitant buyers, those who need just a little more push before they will buy. Don't confuse these people with the people who really want to see a greater display of your wares. These hesitant people will say:

"Well, it looks nice, but *I don't know.*"
"That's a little more than *I thought* of paying."
"Isn't that pretty expensive?"
"Is that the *best* you can do?"
"Do many people buy this make?"

These people want you to "sell" them a little harder. Their statements, as you can see, are weak. After taking the temperature of a person and getting one of these remarks, drive for a close. The sale is practically made!

DON'T SIDE-STEP CRITICISM

If, when taking the temperature, you draw out a criticism or an argument, *don't side-step it,* and don't deny it bluntly and point blank. Here is what to say:

"I'm glad you brought up that point. I was just going to explain it."

"I was coming to that. But first let me explain this feature."

Agree with the customer *first – then* turn him around *afterwards.*

If the prospect says: "Well, it does look nice, but I don't know."

You say: "It is nice, and it suits your needs," and so on. If the customer says: "That's more than I had thought of paying."

Agree and say: "It is a good model, just let me show you why I think it will suit your purpose."

If the customer says: "It is pretty expensive, isn't it?" Agree and say: "It is a fine instrument, madam, and I want to show you why."

Then go right on demonstrating.

Another good rule to remember is: *Sum up the benefits!* After outlining the benefits and advantages of what you are selling, *sum them up,* and conclude your sale by saying:

"Since there are three in your family, and since you want a

mixer that your husband can use for drinks and you can use to mash vegetables, extract orange juice, and use for all forms of beating purposes – this is the mixer you will find most beneficial, don't you agree?"

Another simple summarizing phrase is:

"Because *in your particular case*, etc..."

Always be sure you classify the customer properly as to his or her needs. If a customer is looking around for a topcoat, let us say, for her child, don't try to sell her an overcoat. Find the customer's *needs* before you sell or display. *Inquire before you unload your sales barrage!* And sum up the customer's NEEDS as well as the BENEFITS they will receive from what you are selling!

Always be sure, during the sale, to take the "temperature" of the customer, to make certain that you are on the right track, that you won't oversell, and that you will sell the customer what is on his mind.

Doctors take temperatures – why not you?

CHAPTER 13

SENTENCES THAT TELL YOU THE OTHER PERSON IS "SOLD"

> *Every good salesman instinctively – or consciously – looks for the signals that tell him the other person has been "sold" and that the time has come for him to ask for the money or the signature.*

The more experienced and observant you are, the quicker you will detect these signals. When you see the signal, don't fail to reach out and GRAB THE BRASS RING. To keep on talking and selling once the "buying signal" has been flashed is poor salesmanship, and you will talk yourself right out of the sale.

Here are some good buying signals to watch for:

"How can I keep it bright and shiny?"

"Can it be dry cleaned?"

"Will ordinary polish be satisfactory?"

"Can it be used by two or more people?"

"Is this the best price I can get?"

"Will it scratch or get out of order easily?"

"Do you sell extra parts?"

"Do you deliver?"

"How long before I can get this model delivered?"

"When could you send it out to my home?"

"Is this the very latest model?"

When the "buying signal" is flashed, don't continue to sell. You might say something the customer hadn't thought of and start him off on another trend of thought.

WHEN THE BUYING SIGNAL COMES

When the buying signal comes, get out the pen and order pad and drive for the close by some such statement as these:

"Will you take it with you?"
"Will delivery next Thursday be alright?"
"Where shall I deliver it?"
"Have you an account with us?"
"Which policy do you prefer?"
"When could we start?"

Customers may give the "buying flash" *by some action,* instead of by words, such as:

He may reach for his pen or check book.
He may step back to take a better look.
He may scratch his chin in decision.
He may rub off a spot and look at the label.
He may open up some part.
He may sit on the seat.
He may read the literature.
He may start the motor again.
He may turn on the switch.
He may pick up the contract blank.

Whenever the buying flash is SIGNALED, start the close. The end is in sight. Don't continue talking about the sale *but about the terms.*

A good influencer of people watches for the "sold signal" and stops when he gets it!

THE ART OF QUOTING PRICE

Many a sale has been lost because the price was fumbled, spoken in a hesitant manner, or hurled at the prospect indelicately. There is a definite art in quoting price. Learn this art.

When you lose a sale, it may be because you did not justify price. You failed to make the "sizzle" so strong that price was less and less important.

Many "walk outs" and many lost interviews are due to failure to make price seem small in importance to results and owner benefits. Many sales are lost because the other person "stalled" us out of the sale, and we failed to keep on selling until the buying signal was flashed and the brass ring came in view.

AVOID "PRICE" TOO EARLY

Avoid an early question of price. Say, "I am coming to price, but first let me show you this feature." Or say, "First let me show you this." Or, "I am glad you brought up price, for I have a surprise for you. First, though, let me show you another benefit you will receive."

If price is discussed before the prospect desires the product, price means nothing.

Avoid the expression, "How much?" Do this by keeping the sale moving swiftly down the road of interest, of values, of results, of benefits and advantages. Make it a parade of emotional interest.

Never pretend you failed to hear price. This will cause price to rise from a molehill to a mountain in the mind of the prospect. Meet it at once. Very often when the customer says, "How much?" you can answer indirectly by saying, "You can get them in several prices, but first let me show you our new Dirt Finder." Or you can reply, "It depends on which model will serve your purpose best. Now let me show you the features of our two models."

Let me repeat: When you do quote price, don't stop dramatically. Keep on talking. Price will then pass away into interest. Dramatic pauses after a price is quoted will cause the price to be highlighted.

WEEKLY PAYMENTS SEEM LESS

It is often best to break price down into the small weekly payment, rather than to give the total lump sum.

If the article or sales package you are selling has "extras," quote them in the one price. Don't quote a price for the article, and then the price for the extras. Give one price for all. If necessary, later on, inform the customer she can buy the main article or gadget and get the extras later on.

Never quote too high a price, or too low. Strike a happy medium. Too high a price scares many a customer, as well as too low a price. Show a higher-priced item or a lower-priced one, depending on the customer's reaction to the medium price.

When the customer tells you, "The price is too high," say,

"It may seem high, but it is the finest you can buy." Or agree that the price is high and then outline two or three exclusive "sizzles" that will justify the high price. It is often good psychology to say, "Yes, the price is high, but worth it – for you get this feature exclusively on this cleaner. It is not found on any other make. It is worth the difference in cost, isn't it?"

SELL "SAVINGS," NOT "COST"

Whenever possible show that the article SAVES upkeep costs. You can say:

"The first price is high, but it will save you electricity."
"Yes, but it saves rugs, electricity, and your back."
"Price is relative, madam, to the benefits you get."

Many a price objection is given by a wife to get your answers to fortify herself against her husband; and the same applies to a husband.

Give the customer reasons why the price is high – so she can use these reasons on her mate, father, mother, or boss. Give her ammunition to use to justify her decision to buy.

HELP CUSTOMERS MAKE DECISIONS

Give the customers help. They need it to make decisions.

Help the customer make up her mind. Make the decision for this hesitant customer by giving her reasons for buying what you want to sell her. Often we can get a quick decision by moving the article to some other part of the store, or by showing the silver on a table set up with a table cloth, or by showing the coat on a model, or by showing the car out in the street, away from other models.

When price is the objection, state the objection, make sure it is the ONLY objection, and then set about to show that price is small after all, and close on this key issue.

Say, "Is the price your *only* reason for not buying?" Get the customer to agree that it is, and then show the savings in maintenance, in electricity, in upkeep, in gasoline mileage, and so on.

Often when price is the big obstacle, a review of the owner benefits will make the price seem reasonable after all. When price is quoted, review the benefits, and the price diminishes.

"WHY DO YOU THINK THE PRICE IS HIGH?"

A good "Tested Selling Sentence" to use when price is brought up as the main objection is, "Why do you think the price is high?" This causes the objector to try to explain why he thinks the price is high. It puts him on the defensive. He finds it difficult to tell you why. It gives you time to think. And in many cases when he hears his reason, it is so humble, simple, and ridiculous-sounding that he is sorry he brought it up, and he will often say, "Oh, I guess the price is all right after all. Wrap it up."

That "why" system is effective. Try it to meet any kind of objection. It is a hard one for the prospect to overcome. Get the customer to tell you why the price is too high. You then have something on which to continue the sale. Always get the customer's alibis or excuses.

The art of quoting price is simple once you have mastered these few simple rules. Price is the most important objection to overcome in any sale, and if you are a good closer you will be a winner!

Smooth out the way you quote price. Don't bring the fountain pen and pad into sudden view. Be tactful. This is the critical part of any sale.

Learn this technique of quoting price. It will pay you BIG returns.

The selling word is always mightier than the price tag.

CHAPTER 14

TESTED SENTENCES THAT MAKE
THE OTHER PERSON SAY "YES"

> *Make it easy for the buyer to agree and say "Yes."*
> *How a porter does it. How to do it on "call-backs."*

I was rushing down to Philadelphia the other day with my grip in my hand. When I was half way across the large foyer of Pennsylvania Station, a smiling porter pointed to my bag. At the same time he said, "Which train are you catching?"

Thinking the schedules might have been changed, I informed him I was catching the ten o'clock express. Reaching for my bag, the porter said, "I'll get you *direct* to the *right* platform *quickly.*"

"Fine!" was my reply.

While sitting in the train I realized that the porter had used a surefire sales sentence on me. He got a tip. I got to the train quickly. We both profited.

But suppose that the porter had approached me with the usual, "Carry your bag?" I would have said, "No," because it is light, and there is no need for a man to run after me with such a small bag. He was more subtle, however. Years of using words and techniques on people had taught this porter the best language to use to make it easy for people to say "Yes."

Down at our corner grocery store in Forest Hills, Long Island, the other day, a woman entered the store and asked for

Lux Soap, which comes in two sizes, large and small. The grocer knows that if he asked the woman, "Large or small size?" she would often say, "Oh, small is all right. I can always come back for more."

"TESTED SELLING" IN GROCERIES

Unfortunately, after she runs out of soap the next time, she may be going to some other store, and that store gets the sale. It is always good to get the business while it is in your hand. Therefore, the grocery clerk made it easy for the woman to say "Yes," by the simple sentence, "The family *economical* size, madam?"

The woman said, "Oh, yes, the economical size. I always buy *economically.*"

The woman asks for a pound and a half of steak. Now as skillful as grocery and meat men are, at times they over-cut. When this occurs, I have found there are two ways to handle this situation to make it easy for the woman to buy the over-cut.

In this instance, the meat man over-cut the steak so that it weighed two pounds instead of a pound and a half. If he had said to the woman, in an apologetic manner, "Is that too much?" the woman would probably have said it was. The butcher must then slice off a half pound of the meat. This is hard to do, and it is wasteful, because to sell a thin half-pound slice of steak is not easy.

But the experienced butcher, when he over-cuts, or over-weighs, or over-judges, will always say, "46 cents – will that be enough?"

He seldom mentions the weight – but the price, and adds

that potent selling sentence, "Will that be enough?" And in this case the woman replied, as most will, "Oh, yes, that's quite enough."

SELLING OFFICE SPACE

While I was looking for a new office the other day, I went into 521 Fifth Avenue. I approached the rental man and told him my wants. He showed me several offices, and all the time he was making it easy for me to say "Yes." For instance, he asked me, "Do you like this view of the Hudson River?"

Who wouldn't? I told him I did. He then took me to the other side of the building to another office and again asked me if I liked the view, this time of the East River and Long Island. I did. Suddenly he said, *"Which view do you like better?"*

I thought for a moment. I weighed both views, and then told him that I preferred the view of Long Island. My home was there, and besides, the sun came into the office in the morning when it was least hot.

"Suppose you place your *application* for *this* office, then," said he, tactfully, upon which I realized that I was headed for a dotted line. (I rented the office facing Long Island.)

You can always twist your questions and sales language or social conversations around in such a manner as to make it easy for the other person to say "Yes."

WINNING SOCIAL ARGUMENTS

Even in pleasant arguments you can get positive responses from the other person. You repeat his objections, and ask him, "Is that your *only* reason for not joining our golf club?"

He tells you it is. He *agrees* with you. You have made it easy for him to say "Yes." If you had said to him, "That's a foolish reason for not joining," he would perhaps come back with, "No, sir – it is a GOOD reason – at least to me."

Twist your words in such a manner that they bring out "Yes" answers.

"I'd like to help you build your butter-and-egg business, and you want to do that, don't you?" says our Bickley salesman to his tough prospect, who must say "Yes" to this approach.

"Have you changed your mind about carrying our butter and eggs?" gets a ready "No." No man changes his mind – or wants you to feel he does.

TIMES WHEN YOU WANT A "NO"

Few hotel proprietors want to hear "No" from their guests, yet often they realize that the only way they can improve their service is to find out the things that upset a guest. While developing selling language for Hotels Statler to help improve their service and further refine their contacts with guests, we hit upon this question to get a "Yes" response: *"I am sure* everything is satisfactory with your stay?"

This positive attitude caused many guests to say "Yes," because it was a leading question; and it was much better, we thought, than, "Is everything satisfactory?" which would open the way for some people to complain. But we learned that the sentence "high-pressured" many guests into saying that everything was satisfactory; they would carry their grievances in their minds and on another trip would stay in a competitor's hotel.

It was important to find the annoyances that creep into any

hotel, no matter how carefully it is run. A dripping water faucet, a noisy electric clock, a rattling window – all can be corrected so that they stop annoying the guest and preserve his patronage.

Therefore we constructed the following sentence and tested it. The sentence permitted the guest to offer a complaint if there was one or to say that everything was fine. The sentence was:

"Do you like this room, sir?" ("Do you like the dinner, sir?" and so on.)

It is a simple sentence. Perhaps that is why it is working so successfully.

We tried the sentence, "Is the room satisfactory, sir?" but the word "satisfactory" proved difficult for the bellmen to say, believe it or not!

This incident, of course, indicates there are exceptions to the rule of getting people to say "Yes," for often you really appreciate a sincere "No."

On the whole, however, if you want to get along better with people, especially those you are selling or those you have friendly social arguments with, always bear in mind:

Make it easy for the other person to say "Yes."

WAYS TO PREVENT "NO"

Whenever the other person says "No," you have a mountain to overcome. You have his pride as a hidden objection. You have to unfold his "crossed arms."

In making a "call-back" on a prospect, it is often easy to begin by saying, "Have you changed your mind about my proposition?"

No man wants to have anybody, especially a salesman, change his mind. He likes to "stick by his guns." Oh, yes, some men will change their minds, but they like to think they changed them of their own free will.

If you start an interview with a question the prospect can say "No" to, you are *unnecessarily* handicapping yourself. It is better to say, "Last time I talked with you, your problem was one of price, isn't that so, Mr. Jones?"

He must say "Yes," because you put his own major objection to him. You reworded his objection and "fed" it back to him.

Then you can say, "I have been thinking about the price, and I wonder if we shouldn't look at it from this angle..." You tell him your *new* sales story. His interest is up. You haven't a "No" to surmount.

MEN LIKE TO SAY "NO"

The well-trained Bickley butter-and-egg salesman, as you have read, never greets a Philadelphia grocery prospect with a question like this:

"Need any butter or eggs today?"

He does not give the prospect a chance to say "No." He keeps his man in a "yessing" mood by such statements as this one:

"How'd you like to sell *more* butter and eggs this week, Jim?"

Of course Jim must say "Yes."

Men like to say "No." It is easier to say "No" than "Yes" – because the word "Yes," according to many people, seems to weaken their will, and they like to pride themselves on having a strong will.

BUT DON'T LET HIM SAY "NO"

Marshall Field would always start his trading with salesmen by asking questions, and they were often questions that got "Yes," not "No," answers. He thus learned what was on the other man's mind *first,* and soon had plenty of knowledge on which to trade afterwards.

Emil Ludwig says of Napoleon: "Half of what he achieved was achieved by the Power of Words."

While at the Pyramids, Napoleon said to his army, "Soldiers, forty centuries are looking down on you!" (He was selling the "sizzle.")

He would say, "I will lead you into the most fertile plains of the world. There you will find flourishing cities, teeming provinces."

Another of Napoleon's sayings is, "You will return to your homes, and your neighbors will point you out to one another saying, 'He was with the army in Italy.'"

Napoleon knew the simple art of saying the right thing. He talked about the other person, and would never give his men a chance to say "No" by asking them, "Do you soldiers get enough to eat? Are you satisfied with war?"

According to Elbert Gary, "The average man talks too much, especially if he has a good command of language."

Do your share of the talking only. Let the other fellow talk once in a while. Use questions on him – leading questions that get him talking. Not questions that invite a negative response.

Remember the rule: Don't let the other person say "No."

"BRINGING UP THE SUBJECT"

Very often in the course of persuading the other person you are forced to close the matter for the time being, leaving the situation open for further discussion, or a "call-back," as it is known in salesmanship circles.

The careful interviewer is alert not to "close the incident for all times." To avoid this possibility he usually ends his initial call on his prospect *voluntarily* with some such statement as this:

"It is not necessary for you to make up your mind today. I don't want to rush you. Suppose we drop the matter now, and take it up at another meeting?"

This is often good technique. Few people like to be rushed into a deal, regardless of how small it is. They want time to "think it over," and if you are the first to suggest they "think it over," you have won a point in your favor. Therefore, *be the first to suggest postponement of an interview, if postponement is inevitable.*

DON'T HANG ON

Don't hang on and on, until the other person is forced to manufacture schemes and methods to get rid of you. If he does, you will never be able to get into his presence again for a call-back.

I know a man with an office on Fifth Avenue, who, through his political connections, is forced to meet many people every day. He allows each just about five minutes, and then his secretary appears at his door and says, "Don't forget your appointment, sir!"

This usually causes the visitor to make a quick exit. Remember the old adage of the theater: Stop while they still want more!

IN DEMONSTRATING AUTOMOBILES

If you are trying to convince someone to buy a car take him for a nice ride. Sell him the ride – not the car. But be the first to say, if you see he must take time to think it over, "Now think it over, Mr. Smith. I don't want you to buy my car if you are really not convinced it is the type you want. Suppose you and your wife discuss the matter, and I'll call you up tomorrow?"

This attitude will work magic for you. It will not only win the other person's confidence in you, but will often cause him to make up his mind at once.

How effective these three simple phrases are:

"There's no hurry."
"Take your time."
"Think it over."

You may be squeezing for the sale very hard, but once you show anxiety, the other person puts you on the defensive – which is a difficult side to be on.

THE SCIENCE OF "CALL-BACKS"

The real science of making the call-back is quite simple. You must open your call-back *at the exact place you left off,* which is usually at the one key objection offered by the other person.

If price is the thing that is holding him back, you start right off with the objection by saying, "Last time we talked this matter over, you stated that price was the only thing holding you back. Is that right?"

He starts "yessing" you right away. But you will always get a negative reply by starting out with, "Have you changed your mind?" or "Have you been thinking about my proposition since the last time we met?"

Experience analyzing 105,000 selling phrases and having them tested on close to 19,000,000 people to date has indicated to me that successful call-backs are those made when you begin with the KEY ISSUE.

For instance, say, "The last time we discussed that home on Beaver Street you told me you didn't like the people who lived in the neighborhood, and that was your ONLY REASON for not moving. Is that right?"

They're his own words. He starts by agreeing with you. Now, you have been making some investigations since he saw fit to stand behind this argument, and you begin knocking the props from under his objection by these new facts:

"Did you know that the Vandersplices, the people who own the gold mines in Mexico, are moving into the neighborhood? Did you know that the Browns, who own the department store, have a daughter who lives directly across the street from the house we looked at? And did you know that your golf partner, Jim, was out looking at this development himself last week?"

Gracious – he didn't realize all this. He is forced to admit that this changes the complexion of things. Then you use the famous KEY ISSUE CLOSE, and close on the main objection with this simple formula that applies to the close of any sale or debate or business argument or social discussion you may be in:

"You told me your ONLY REASON for not moving was the fact you felt the people in the neighborhood were not your type. Isn't that true? And now, you agree the people are just the ones you like. That's true, isn't it? So inasmuch as *this was your only reason* for hesitating, and since this reason is no more, when will you move, the first or the fifteenth of next month?"

**Always use words that get the answers you want –
and you will always retain command of the situation!**

CHAPTER 15

MAKING 'EM HIT THE SAWDUST TRAIL FOR YOU

Back to that old fear appeal again. The pastor says, "You will go to Hell!" The quack says, "It will prevent fallen arches and premature old age." The old medicine man with his Indian stooge knew how to play on your fears with his swamp root tonic.

A vacuum cleaner salesman is working hard in Mrs. Jones' home. He has produced eight small piles of dirt from her rug. He knows the woman is becoming nervous and embarrassed by the sight of the dirt he is able to get from her rug. He puts her at ease by saying, "Don't let this dirt embarrass you, Mrs. Jones. Wherever I use this wonderful machine it digs dirt, because only this machine has patented Grit Removers that get the dirt *below the surface,* out of reach of ordinary cleaners. Why only this morning at Mrs. Smith's home I got sixteen piles of dirt!"

That puts her at ease. She has eight piles *less* than Mrs. Smith has!

The salesman notices Mrs. Jones children. He plays on her fear for her children's health by saying, "Where do your children play on rainy days, Mrs. Jones?"

"In the house, of course," she replies to the leading question, wondering.

"Then this is your child's rainy day playground, Mrs. Jones!" he says, pointing to the eight piles of dirt!

Gracious – she hadn't realized that this dirt pile *was* her child's "rainy day playground" – his "indoor sand piles." Those were "dynamite words." They EXPLODED inside her with a bang – because they were pre-tested!

"HELL" – ONCE WORLD'S GREATEST FEAR APPEAL

After my talk recently before the Buffalo Rotary Club, a well-known pastor approached me and said, "We used to keep people coming to church on Sunday with the word 'Hell,' but today it has lost its effectiveness."

How true. The word "Hell" has become trite. It once stood for brimstone and fire. But it does no more.

I have often watched Billy Sunday "trade" on the word "Hell." He used it to get people to hit his famous sawdust trail. But Billy Sunday's technique has gone with the cigar and the derby salesman.

Yet there are other fears that will keep the children from going to the movies with the collection money and that will keep dad off the golf links until after church. One church advertises: "Your Sins – and How to Overcome Them."

The pastor realizes he is in competition with the press agents for golf courses and movies, with automobile salesmen, and with the health appeals of the beach owners. He is watching his words!

THE OLD MEDICINE MAN

The medicine man can open his business on any street corner, and within three minutes he has customers. Why? Because of the words he shouts into the crowds, words that capture your ears, that turn your eyes to what he is doing. Ten-second sales messages. His leading questions are:

"Do you feel tired at times? Do you feel like giving up? Does your back ache at four o'clock every afternoon? Do your feet hurt you every night? Can you see that bird on the top of this building? Can you jump over a fence three feet high? If you can't, then step right up here gentlemen, and let me show you something that will put pep into your old blood, that will make you feel like a day in spring, a trip through the mountains, as refreshed as an ocean breeze."

The medicine man is trading on your fears and on your desires, alike, with leading questions that get him the answers HE wants. He is hitting your basic buying motive number 1: Self-preservation (X)!

You step up to his portable store. You are all eyes and ears. You are skeptical – but not for long when this orator begins to play on your emotions as the harpist plays on the strings of a harp. His words are music to the ears of all "sufferers," especially of imaginary ills.

"QUICK RELIEF" –
THE DRUG STORE'S
BEST WORDS

Step into any People's, Economical-Cunningham, or Pennsylvania Drug Store where we have installed "Tested

Selling Sentences" principles. You will find two words being used over and over again, "quick relief."

Grandmother has a backache. Dad has a corn. Mother has a headache. Each steps up to the drug counter. The druggist places a prescribed package in front of each, and says simply, "These will give all of you *quick relief.*"

Each buys because that is what each wanted most for his ailment, "quick relief." Look at all the signs today shouting variations of these two words.

You see: *"Instant* relief from headaches," *"quick* relief for corns, *"prompt* relief from heart burn," and so on.

These two words are making millions for drug manu-facturers and for drugstore owners everywhere – QUICK RELIEF!

It is the appeal to our self-preservation emotions; the desire to get our health back again, to be our "normal selves"; the fear of losing our health, our youth, of getting gray hair, wrinkles, or acid stomach.

But don't OVERDO this fear appeal! And be sure when you say it will give "quick relief," that you are HONEST!

MAKING UP YOUR MIND

Several years ago, the Cunningham Drug Stores of Detroit, in the person of Mr. Nat Shapiro, came to our laboratory. His extensive chain of Midwestern stores was overstocked with products for the feet.

"How can we introduce these products to men and women?" he asked me.

Fifty-five customer approaches were tabulated for his use. One after another of these sentences was tried, until this subtle, indirect, harmless, split-second attention-getter was success-fully created:

"Are you on your feet much?"

Here was a leading question to which nine out of every twelve people would remark that they were. All of us feel we are on our feet more than we should be or wish to be. With this wonderful opening, then, the salespeople in this chain of stores would say:

"This will ease your feet. It is made ESPECIALLY for people who are on their feet a lot."

Customers would pick up the product. The appeal was directed to them. It was directed to their instinct of self-preservation. It shot by their natural resistances, and hit those tiny "mental pocketbooks" inside the emotional part of their brains. Hundreds of packages were sold the first week! Again the right words – spoken at the right time!

People WILL hit the sawdust trail for you if you motivate them by first appealing to them emotionally.

A SELL-OUT IN TOOTHBRUSHES

Bloomingdale, Abraham & Straus, Stern Brothers, William Taylor, and Saks 39th Street department stores all sold out of toothbrushes some months ago by the simple application of a sentence TESTED to capture the fleeting interest of customers in ten seconds.

The old expressions – "Need any toothbrushes today?" – "How ya fixed for toothbrushes?" – "We have a special on today," – and so on – failed to sell the brushes, a staple item. People seldom stock up in toothbrushes. It is a "necessity" item.

One day the clerks in these stores were instructed by one of our staff to approach each customer who had made a regular purchase with this statement:

"Have you ever used a SCIENTIFIC toothbrush, madam?"

The customer would ask what a "scientific toothbrush" was, and the salesperson would hold up the favorite brush and say:

"The bristles are ADJUSTED to clean BETWEEN the teeth!"

These "arrow-like words" shot to the proper niche of the brain, and sales increased.

In fact, for the first time in the history of each one of these stores, the toothbrushes were sold completely out of stock in less than a week – a testimonial deluxe to the power of "Tested Selling Sentences." Just two sentences made customers hit the old sawdust trail for toothbrush manufactures and retailers – and helped customers have finer, well-cleaned teeth!

A COUNTER SIGN THAT SELLS

One day Doctors Beaver and Gibbs, of the People's Drug Stores of Washington, informed us they wanted to get men to begin using an underarm deodorant to avoid perspiration. If men could be induced to use this product, a brand new market would be developed overnight.

We told them it would be easy. We would instruct the salesgirls to have their customers teach their husbands the many advantages of a deodorant. Then the bottle would be used twice as fast in the home, and the woman would be back to the store twice as frequently.

A fine theory, but what a sad experience! The salesgirl

would say to a buyer of a deodorant, "Why not teach your husband its many advantages, madam?"

The customer would come back with, "What makes you think I have a husband?" Or, "What makes you think he needs it, young lady?"

We then tried several ideas at the cigar counters, man-to-man stuff. But again we experienced difficulty. A man would buy some cigars, and the clerk would say, "How about some deodorant today, sir?"

"No thanks," the man would reply. "My wife uses Flit." He didn't even know what a deodorant was! When he found out, he was insulted, wondering why the clerk suggested it to him!

THE "HE-MAN" APPEAL

Finally we placed a sign on the cigar counter reading: "For Men." In front of the sign we placed a bar of Lifebuoy soap and a bottle of Odorono. The Lifebuoy suggested the use of the Odorono, for men do read the ads of he-men in showers using Lifebuoy. Instinctively they felt the bottle on the counter was for the same purpose. They would shyly pick it up and ask, "What is this?"

The clerk would say: "It's for excessive perspiration!"

The sign stopped four out of every ten men at the cigar counters!

One day we changed the sign to read: "For ACTIVE Men!" Then it stopped six out of ten men; for all men, the short, the lean, the poor, and the wealthy, believing themselves to be active men, would rush to the counter, pick up the bottle, and ask, "What is this?"

Here is proof of the great power of words properly chosen

– even on counter signs!

Look for the "sizzle" in your product; look for the "square clothespin" in whatever you are selling; find the "swamp root"; look for the "Hell"; then remember Wheelerpoint 5, and "Watch Your Bark!"

**That's the simple formula for making people
hit the sawdust trail for you!**

CHAPTER 16

DON'T SELL THE WINE – SELL
THE BUBBLES IN THE GLASS

Hotels Statler makes the first concentrated study in hotel history of effectiveness of words on people. Words that sell the better rooms. Words that sell more wines and food. Selling the view – not the room number. The important "Rule of You" in Hotels and Restaurants. The value of your name.

It is back in the nineties and a group of men saunter to a bar. Joe, the bartender, with his handle-bar mustache, gives the boys a smile and opens his conversation with the familiar, "What'll you gents have?"

They call for a round of drinks, and Joe places his best brand of whiskey on the bar and lines up the glasses in front of them.

Now, the technique of serving people at the bar falls into two classifications, with one group of bartenders letting guests pour their own drinks and the other pouring the drinks themselves. Which is the better principle? Which is the most profitable to the bar?

A study of these questions for Mr. Frank A. McKowne, progressive president of Hotels Statler, along with a survey on how to brighten up the language used by all other hotel employees, brought out some interesting sidelights in human behaviorism.

LET THEM POUR THEIR OWN

The average bottle of spirits contains about twenty-two drinks of the size that the bartender pours. He can "rim" the glass, and he is expected to do so. If he permits you to pour your own drink, however, and most drinkers like to do this, it is difficult for you to rim the glass as the bartender does. In fact, it would be very impolite to do so; it would appear quite "Scotch" to your friends. Therefore you pour the drink to within about a quarter of an inch of the top of the glass. This is the widest part of the glass. This quarter of an inch saving on twenty-two drinks, at 40¢ per drink, amounts to a total savings per bottle of anywhere from 75¢ to $1.25! That means the hotel can get an approximate average of $1.00 *more per bottle* if it is gracious enough to permit the guests to pour their own drinks. Try this technique in your own home, or watch it in practice at some bar.

Of course, in certain districts where guests would not hesitate to put three fingers around the top of the glass and pour a drink to their finger tops, this psychology won't work profitably!

THE "RULE OF YOU" IN HOTELS

Your name is the thing you like to hear most, and it is the greatest selling aid a salesman has.

We have helped to devise many interesting methods by which employees in Hotels Statler can learn your name very quickly and pass it on to other employees. For instance, the desk clerk reads your name as you sign it on the register.

He says, "I have a pleasant room overlooking the Hudson, *Mr. Smith. You* will enjoy the view!"

The bellman standing by hears your name. He takes your bag and says, "This way, *Mr. Smith.*" He gets to the elevator and announces you to the elevator boy by saying, "This is a fine day, isn't it, *Mr. Smith?*"

The elevator boy hears your name. If there is a floor clerk, the bellman walks up to her to get the key to your room, and says, "Key 808 please for *Mr. Smith.*"

The floor clerk hears your name. So on and on, from the time you enter a hotel until you leave, the "Rule of You" will be put into practice, for there is nothing more important than the sound of your own name.

SELLING GLASSES OF BUBBLES

One of the tasks assigned to us by Mr. J. L. Hennessy, the able vice president in charge of catering of this great chain of Statler Hotels, was to study the habits of people eating in restaurants to ascertain how to introduce them to the fine art of drinking wines.

We discovered that there are many reasons why wine was not being ordered. The waiter would mechanically hand the wine list to the guest after seating him. The guest was in a flutter, having walked across a busy hotel room. He was busy adjusting himself to his surroundings. The wine list was merely a blur to him. Should he be able to concentrate on the list, he was afraid to pronounce some of the wine names that were new to him. He didn't know whether to say "Chateau E-kem," or "Chateau Y-quem." He didn't want a waiter to smile at a wrong pronunciation. If the bewildered guest felt confident he could pronounce the name, he was afraid it might be the wrong wine for the occasion. This again caused him to hesitate in ordering a wine. He usually closed the issue with, "Gimme a glass of ale."

We instructed the waiters not to hand a wine list to the guest, but to say, "Would you care for some Chateau E-kem with your order, sir?" The man heard the right pronunciation, and he knew the waiter had without doubt picked the right wine for the dish. He would order the wine. This idea worked expertly until one man thought Chateau E-kem was *a gravy* for his roast, and a woman thought it was a new *salad dressing!*

We kept testing until we made another interesting discovery. Americans most often identify wines by the colors red and white. They like that "red wine I get at the Italian spaghetti house," or that "white wine Aunt Emma serves at Christmas time."

"RED OR WHITE, SIR?"

So the waiters were instructed to approach guests with, "Would you care for a red wine with your roast, sir?" If the dish required a white wine, they would say, "Would you care for a white wine with your fish, sir?"

Then it was found that if an American likes a red wine, he drinks it with any kind or type of food. If the waiter suggested the white wine as being proper, certain guests demanded to know if the hotel was "out of red wine."

How to find out if a guest was a red wine or a white wine drinker? We went back to Wheelerpoint 4: Don't ask IF – ask WHICH. The waiter would say, "Would you care for a red or a white wine with your dinner, sir?"

The guest could make his choice. This approach worked until just recently, when a guest in the Boston Statler Hotel, according to Messrs. Stanbro and Cushing, co-managers, wanted to know, "Is it on the house?"

We immediately added the word "order" to the sentence, and sales of wines have increased from 2¢ to 4¢ per guest. The "Tested Selling Sentence" is now:

"Would you care to ORDER a red or a white wine with your dinner, sir?" Such is the power of ONE WORD – provided it is properly chosen.

FINDING THE "FIRST TIMERS"

It is important for a hotel to know if you are a "first timer." If so, the hotel desires to familiarize you with its many services.

The problem of how to find out if a guest was a first timer in Statler Hotels was given to us as part of our assignment by Mr. John C. Burg, personnel director. With the help of Mr. Burg and the Pennsylvania Hotel staff in New York, we set about making this study. As a test we instructed the bellboys to say, when they were carrying a guest's bags to his room, "Is this the FIRST TIME you've been with us, Mr. Brown?"

If it was, the bellboy would tell the guest how to get radio music in the room, how to get ice water, and how to use the Servidor and other Statler features. If the guest informed him this was not his first time, the bellboy would not annoy him with this recital of features that were perhaps well known to the regular guest.

It was a fine system, but it *failed* to work!

The first day we found ten guests who complained, "You fellows ought to know me by this time. I've been coming to this hotel for years. If this is all the impression I make on you fellows, I'll change hotels."

Therefore we changed the expression to, "Have you been with us RECENTLY, Sir?"

The "Tested Selling Sentence" now works successfully, showing that the right formation of words gets the right responses from people. *It is all in how you say it.*

THE TECHNIQUE OF THE DOORMAN

The doorman in front of any hotel or restaurant is the king of the hotel. He is usually a pompous person, dressed up like a Mexican general. He makes the first impression for the hotel, because he is the first person you see when you visit a hotel. If this "ten-second person" makes a poor impression, your impression of the entire hotel is weakened.

A study of the Statler Hotel doormen brought out some important observations. If the doorman holds his hand out, palm up, to a woman guest to assist her out of an automobile, she may trip accidentally and cause him to press her hand a little too tightly, which she is apt to resent. The alert doorman, therefore, will always put his hand inside the automobile, *palm down,* fist clenched, giving the lady an opportunity to *lift herself* out of the seat, with no chance of an accidental squeezing of her hand. The doorman then counts the baggage and says: "Three bags, madam?"

She nods yes, or tells him there is a small black bag in the dark corner on the floor. Many guests leave baggage in taxicabs, but this simple statement on the part of doormen is proving very valuable to Statler Hotels in eliminating the danger of lost baggage.

WHICH TYPE ARE YOU?

We have told you that one secret of choosing the right words to get proper responses from people is to know at which basic motive (X, Y, Z) to direct your words.

Studying human nature as it enters a restaurant in a large Statler Hotel for breakfast has taught us there are three types of American breakfast eaters at which a waiter must direct his words. The first is the fellow who has lost his appetite. He needs a good waiter with the power to make the guest's mouth water with highly descriptive words. Good waiters will suggest, "A glass of chilled tomato juice, sir, with a dash of lemon and Worcestershire sauce?"

The second type of breakfast eater is the "morning grouch." He comes storming in. He was awake all night. Or he has indigestion. Or he cut himself while shaving. The alert waiter says nothing to him, not even good morning, unless it is quite unobtrusively spoken. But he gets rolls and butter in front of the "morning grouch" in a hurry, because with a roll in his mouth "the fellow finds it hard to complain."

The third type of guest is familiar to all of us. He comes flying into the restaurant. His necktie is twisted. He flings his hat to the waiter. He is the guest who is always late for an appointment – always in a hurry. *He wants three-minute eggs in two minutes!* Waiters know better than to tell the gentleman this is an impossible feat. Instead, they hustle about with great motion. This technique satisfies the guest that he is getting quick service.

Study again the three basic emotions – X, Y, and Z – then direct your statements to hit the mark, especially if you are in a business that depends on servicing the public efficiently and unobtrusively.

A BAKED IDAHO POTATO
WITH SWEET BUTTER

Don't sell the steak – sell the sizzle. It is the sizzle that makes the guest's mouth water, not the cow!

Don't sell potatoes – sell a baked Idaho potato with sweet melted butter.

It's the bubbles on the wine that make the eyes sparkle in anticipation.

On three occasions lately we sold out completely the "chef's special in the Cafe Rouge of the Hotel Pennsylvania in New York within two hours' time, by use of tested descriptive words. For instance, the fish was not just "baked fish" to Mr. Henessey, but "fish baked in the Back Bay manner," and the stew was not an ordinary stew, but "beef pie a la mode."

"Would you care to order a Martini or a Manhattan, sir?" has increased sales of these two drinks in all the Statler Hotels.

How much better are these suggested sentences than the obsolete approach used by Joe, the old-time bartender, "What'll you gents have?"

"LISTENING A LITTLE CLOSER"

I always wondered why I enjoyed the company of Grand-pop Strobel so much. He would sit for hours listening to me tell him about the things I was doing, and he never seemed bored.

A lot of people, especially complaint managers in organizations, have this knack of letting you do all the talking. Once in a while we catch ourselves being "coaxed on," and, remembering the Rule of "You-ability," we start the other person talking.

Then, too, there are some people who listen to us, but when we look into their eyes *directly,* we immediately see that their supposed interest in us is an acquired act, and that in reality their thoughts are far away.

These people are like the famous "Yes people," who keep saying "Yes" – "How interesting" – "So exciting" – "Is that so?" – "Hum, what do you think of that," but who never buy. These people are professional listeners. They know the art of letting the other person do the talking, but somehow or other we quickly "catch on" to these professionals and make up our minds we will not get caught in their trap again.

GRANDPOP STROBEL
KNOWS HIS STUFF

But not Grandpop Strobel. He really listens, especially when Grandma Strobel talks, and I have always wondered what his charm was for getting people to do the talking while he sat peacefully back and smoked his pipe, resting his vocal chords and winning new friends.

One day I found the answer through accidentally hearing someone on the street, a mere passerby, say, "He has a habit of 'listening a little closer,' if you get what I mean."

I got what he meant. Grandpop "listened a little closer."

You have seen this type of salesman. He bends toward you

physically, and leans on you mentally, with every word you utter. He is "with you" every moment, nodding and smiling at the right times. He "listens a little closer" which is the best way I know of describing why people like to tell Grandpop about the things they are doing, and why they tell Grandpop all their troubles.

This is a fine art for a salesman to acquire, that of "listening a little closer." I like salesmen who "listen well" to what I am saying.

Therefore, one way to raise your selling average is to "listen a little closer" – if you see what I mean, if you see what I see in Grandpop Strobel. It is a sound rule to follow for social and business success, especially if you are a hotel or restaurant owner, or if you are on the complaint staff of your business.

"Listen a little closer!"

CHAPTER 17

DON'T SELL THE SARDINES –
SELL THE SOMERSAULT

> *A grocery chain sells sardines. It increases sales of potatoes. It knows the value of ten-second sales messages. It tells owner benefits. It gives proof. It sells the "sizzle" – not the cow.*

Several years ago I addressed the Cleveland Rotary Club on the subject of "Word Magic." It is my custom to start my talk with my own ten-second opener to catch the fleeting interest of the audience, so they will forget their desserts, and stop rattling their forks. I usually say:

"What makes people buy things?

"Have you ever bought a bright red necktie with a lot of wild-eyed dragons on it, and later on said to yourself, 'What in thunder did that sales clerk ever say to make me buy such a thing?'"

Now it so happened that Mr. Harry Simms, president of the Cleveland Rotary, was wearing such a necktie that day. The audience laughed considerably, and Mr. Simms began thinking very seriously. He was president of Chandler & Rudd, a chain of quality stores in Cleveland. He invited me to his office after the talk and gave me several problems to solve for him, among which was a need for a plan to sell his higher-priced sardines.

THEY WERE TURNED UPSIDE DOWN

I analyzed his customers and found that they were like those everywhere in the world. When they were shown Rudd sardines and told the price was 25¢ a can, they would say, "What is the difference between your 25¢ sardines and the 10¢ brands sold at the chains?"

The Rudd salespeople tried in vain to paint a picture to convince the women that their sardines were better.

I analyzed both brands. I measured the two kinds of sardines as to length and counted them. Rudd sardines did taste a little better, but it was hard to convey this taste difference quickly to customers.

One day I noticed a grocery clerk turning the boxes of sardines upside down on the shelf. I asked him why. He told me that the purpose was to start the oil, which settles in the bottom of the can, seeping through the sardines to keep them from drying up in the cans. He stated, very convincingly, that sardines that were constantly bathed in the olive oil inside the can tasted better, looked better, and were enjoyed much more by the one who ate them.

What a fine sales idea! But how could the story be told in ten seconds in a busy store?

SELLING THE SOMERSAULT

A sentence finally popped to life. The clerks were instructed to say, "Rudd sardines are turned UPSIDE DOWN once a month!"

This simple statement caused the customers' curiosity to respond. They would inquire why the sardines were turned upside down, and the clerk would tell them this interesting story.

The story made the women's mouths water. They bought them. When hubby exclaimed, as he always does, about the high cost of food, his wife would tell him the story of the sardines "that were turned upside down once a month."

She sold him the somersault – not the sardines!

He too responded – and the sardines DID seem to taste 15¢ better per can!

For the first time in the history of Chandler & Rudd these expensive sardines were sold completely out of stock inside of two weeks – a store record.

Motto: Look for the SOMERSAULT IN YOUR product!

SELLING IMITATION VANILLA

No woman will risk the affections of her husband by baking him a cake with imitation vanilla, even though the imitation is 8¢ cheaper than the real vanilla.

Yet the imitation is very good. In fact, Kroger's chain of grocery stores in upper Ohio thought enough of a certain brand of imitation vanilla to buy thousands of bottles, only to find they would not sell.

Mr. Charles McCahill, vice president of the *Cleveland News,* was endeavoring to influence Kroger's to use his newspaper instead of his competitor's. As a final inducement he offered to employ our institution to devise "Tested Selling Sentences" to help Kroger's sell their imitation vanilla and other slow-moving items.

After a prolonged study of the product, and after discarding hundreds of sentences and techniques that failed to hold up under actual tests behind the counters, we again employed the principle of getting the product into the hands of the customer, where it will sell twenty-one times faster.

The clerks in this great chain were instructed, after every regular sale to a woman, to remove the cork of the imitation vanilla, *smell of it first,* and as they held the bottle toward the customer say, *"Hasn't this a fine vanilla flavor?"*

The women were prompted (monkey see, monkey do) to smell of the imitation vanilla, which really had a strong, full-bodied vanilla aroma, and, like many imitations, appeared to be ever better than the original. They would remark on the fine, strong fragrance, and when they read on the label that the bottle contained imitation vanilla, they could hardly believe their eyes. On finding that it was 8¢ cheaper than the real vanilla, they were tempted to buy it.

They received the owner benefit (A) very tactfully. The smell was the proof (B).

Our records show that Kroger's increased sales of this product ten percent and that the Cleveland News got the Kroger account on an equal copy basis!

What a result to achieve with six simple little words!

COLD GROWN POTATOES

Chandler & Rudd increased the sale of potato salad by this simple statement to the "what's-the-difference-in-price" customer:

"It is made from COLD GROWN potatoes!"

Rudd potatoes, they explained to the women, came from "Maine, the coldest state in the Union, where potatoes are grown firm and meaty because of the low temperatures." The sale of Quaker Oats increased ten percent when the clerks used this as their opening statement: "Have you served oatmeal recently, Mrs. Jones?"

This tactful reminder to buy Quaker Oats is just a simple statement, but like most effective sentences, the simpler the sentence the more effective the results.

Fancy phrases attract attention only to the phrases or to the speaker, not to the product. Coined words amuse you. They seldom sell you.

Big men are simple. Great sales sentences are simple. The salesman who looks like a crack salesman scares his prospect.

Simple expressions sell people faster! Look for the simple sizzles in your sales package.

THREE SENTENCES
THAT SAVED A LIFE

When a rabbi, a priest, a doctor, and a hundred firemen and policemen fail to "sell" a man on life and three sentences convince the man not to commit suicide – that is front page news!

It was front page news recently in newspapers nationally, when a manufacturer, bored with life, went to the roof of a New York hotel and prepared to jump eighteen stories to his death.

He was noticed climbing over the wall to a nine-inch ledge, from which he was going to leap to the street below. A secretary in the hotel screamed, and the man hesitated.

Hotel employees ran out on the roof. They asked the man not to jump, but he kept moving dangerously toward the nine-inch ledge. His mind was shattered.

Records of the incident showed the following conversation and the various underlying appeals used by the many people who, during the eighty-minute roof drama, tried to dissuade the man from taking his life:

SELF-PRESERVATION
RELIGIOUS SENTENCES

RABBI: "It is against your RELIGION to take your own life!"

PRIEST: "Don't do anything you'll REGRET, my good man!"

DOCTOR: "You will seriously INJURE yourself if you jump!"

FIREMEN: "Don't jump – get back – you'll fall!"

POLICE: "Get off that ledge – wanna get killed!"

Sensing that these appeals to self-preservation and the man's religion were failing, and that he was walking closer to the ledge, preparing to jump the eighteen stories to his death, Miss Diane Gregal, vice president of Tested Selling Institute, who was called to the scene, used these appeals:

PERSONAL COMFORT APPEALS

"Shall I get you a cup of coffee?"

"Would you like a glass of wine?"

When these appeals to the man's personal comforts likewise failed, and as he was about to jump, Miss Gregal began to appeal to the man's VANITY!

VANITY APPEALS

"You look SILLY perched upon that ledge!"

"Suppose your wife sees you in that RIDICULOUS place!"

"Better get down at once BEFORE she sees what a FOOL you are making of yourself!"

It was interesting to the many spectators to see the man begin to brush off his clothing and arrange his hat upon hearing the words *silly, ridiculous,* and *fool.* Evidently, he could withstand every appeal but that of appearing "silly," especially to his wife, for he walked peacefully off the dangerous ledge to safety.

CHAPTER 18

FIVE LITTLE WORDS THAT SOLD A MILLION GALLONS OF GASOLINE

> *The selling word is mightier than the price tag. With words we govern people. A million people every week buy gasoline and oil because of certain tested words they ear from the Man at the Pump.*

My dad owned a gasoline station near Highland Park in Rochester, New York. On Saturdays and Sundays I would help him sell oil. One day a gasoline salesman from Standard Oil approached me. He asked me, "What do you say to sell gasoline to motorists?"

I had no particular statement, so I told him: "Sometimes I ask people if they want five or ten, other times I just say, 'how many today?'"

The salesman said, "The next motorist who comes in, say this to him: 'Shall I fill it up?'"

I used the sentence, and the motorist told me to fill his tank. *I sold fifteen gallons instead of the usual five or ten.*

What a surefire method of getting tanks filled up! The sentence worked, and has been working successfully now for twenty years.

RECENT EXPERIMENTS
FOR TEXAS OIL

Recently I had the pleasure of making a survey for the Pocahontas Oil Corporation of Ohio and the Texas Oil Company to find the best modern words and techniques to use in influencing motorists to purchase more petroleum products.

People have a bad habit of letting things go that need attention. Cars that need greasing never get the grease until some alert station attendant tactfully reminds the motorists.

Our research at the point of sale brought out many interesting things. First, my old favorite, "Shall I fill it up?" doesn't work anymore. You see, there are too many old cars with twenty-gallon tanks on the market today. Years ago the rich man owned the big car and the poor man owned the little car. Nowadays a poor man can buy a good used car once owned by a wealthy person and get good use out of it.

Picture, therefore, the hundreds of cases such as this: Tony Pasquale buys an old car for $50. He wants the big "hack" just to drive to and from his girl's house. He drives into a gasoline station. He has two dollars, his best girl, *and a twenty-gallon tank.* The attendant says, "Shall I fill it up?"

Tony is embarrassed. He tells the attendant to go ahead, but he slyly puts three fingers over the side of the car to indicate that is all he wants.

"Shall I fill it up?" needs revision. In fact, our recent changes of the expression indicate that the new "gasoline approach" we are developing will prove even more effective than the famous old one that has sold a million gallons of gasoline.

"HOW ABOUT SOME OIL?"

The "how-about-some-oil" salesman sells little oil. He annoys you with his, "Shall I check your oil?" He is one of the high-pressure salesmen we are trying to convert.

Mr. H. W. Dodge, vice president of the Texas Company, called me to his offices in the Chrysler Building one day. He explained that the New Texas Oil would be put on the market soon, and that his 45,000 dealers needed something definite to say to motorists to introduce this new oil. Mr. Dodge realized that his best product will pass unnoticed before the eyes of the public unless certain words are used to describe it effectively and dramatically. Therefore, a study was made of the habits of American motorists.

It was found that they had a habit, born during the depression, of saying "No" before thinking. Ask them if they needed any oil, and they'd say "NO." Ask them if they had seen the New Texaco Oil, and they'd say, "No – not interested – just five gallons of gasoline, please."

Out of a hundred methods of approaching motorists at the pumps while they were getting gasoline, to sell them the New Texaco Oil, this statement proved best (perhaps it was used on you)

"Is your oil at *proper driving level?"*

These seven little words were used by *45,000* Texaco dealers in one week on a total of nearly *485,000* motorists. It helped the dealers get under a quarter of a million hoods. *It exposed these Texaco dealers to a potential quarter of a million sales of the new oil in one week.*

It was a ten-second attention-getter that succeeded *58* percent of the time, because it capitalized on the word "NO!" It invited a "NO" – for in this case "NO" meant "YES!" The fear appeal again.

"YOUR RIGHT FRONT TIRE, SIR"

It is a proved fact that, if you are like most people, you will drive your car until the tires literally fall off, unless some alert station attendant reminds you of the dangers that confront you.

He will step up to your car, wipe off the windshield, and as he is doing so will remark about the weather or a topic of current interest. Then he will walk in front of the car and inspect your tires as he checks your water supply. Should one of your tires be worn, he will say:

"Your right front tire, sir, is badly worn. Just look at this spot."

He gets you out of the seat where you can "look at the spot" and where he can talk with you better. The sale is on the way. His chance of increasing his business is very promising. He watches *your* tires – and he watches *his* words.

YOUR WORN-OUT WINDSHIELD WIPER

Windshield wipers are like shoe laces. They stay broken a long time before you replace them; that is, unless you are approached by an efficient salesman with the desire to influence you. He has a windshield wiper handy in his pocket. He realizes that any sale is made twenty-one times faster if he can get his goods into his customer's hands for inspection.

Not being a "how-about-it" salesman, he says:

"Feel the TRIPLE EDGE on this wiper, sir."

You do. The wiper is in your hands. He then tells you the

benefits and advantages (A) you will get from a triple bladed windshield wiper. *That simple sentence is tested to sell blades to three out of every fifteen motorists – more on rainy days!*

It's all in how you say it. The selling word is always mightier than the price tag!

"TESTED SELLING" IN LETTERS

Here is perhaps one of the cleverest one-line statements that has ever appeared in a direct-mail letter and, though it appears facetious on the surface, I am told by Henry Hoke, secretary of the Direct Mail Association, that it got results:

JONES INSURANCE COMPANY

Mr. Tom Smith
Flushing, L. I.
New York.

Dear Mr. Smith:

If you can save the small amount of $2.50 per week, you can be insured for life – if you can't, *you are a big sissy!*

Yours very truly,
Jonathan Jones

In all events, this proves one thing: It is important, even in direct mail, to pick out surefire "sizzles" and to make certain they sell the benefits, or the results to be obtained.

A sardine is a sardine, but a sardine that is turned upside down once a month takes on an interesting aspect to women shoppers.

H. GORDON SELFRIDGE SPEAKS

H. Gordon Selfridge, according to B. C. Forbes, once wrote the following statement, which I like very much. It again shows the importance of choosing your words and sentences if you would get along with people – your employers, your employees, your family, or your prospects. Here is Selfridge's interesting statement:

"The boss drives his men; the leader coaches them."

"The boss depends upon authority; the leader on goodwill."

"The boss inspires fear; the leader inspires enthusiasm."

"The boss says 'I'; the leader says 'We'"

"The boss says 'Get here on time'; the leader gets there ahead of time."

"The boss fixes the blame for the breakdown; the leader fixes the breakdown."

"The boss knows how it is done; the leader shows how."

"The boss makes work a drudgery; the leader makes work a game."

"The boss says 'Go'; the leader says 'Let's go.'"

Bloomingdale's Department Store of New York sold furniture polish twice as fast one spring by having the clerk use this opening statement as he held a bottle of their favorite polish toward the customer:

"It cleans and polishes in ONE EASY operation."

The salespeople sold the "operation" – not the polish.

Two follow-up "Tested Selling Sentences" were:

"It will save many a spring backache."

"It will cut your spring house cleaning in HALF!"
On the counter was a "talking sign" that said:

SPRING HOUSECLEANING TIME IS HERE
Get a Bottle of Polish Today!

**There is an art in making words sell – and
it is an art that you can easily acquire
by just a little study of how to
sell the "sizzle" – not the cow!**

CHAPTER 19

DON'T USE WORDS THAT ARE "SHINY IN THE SEAT"

The other person begins to respond with his first "No." But try not to give him a chance to be negative. Avoid trite words that mean nothing. Words that are baggy in the knees lose business. Press up your words. Keep the shine of them.

I often drop into a drug store to get a malted milk. If the clerk can sell me an egg in it, the store will get 5¢ more from me, and I will have a fuller, richer drink, which I like. If the clerk has baggy trousers and baggy words, he'll ignore the good rule of asking leading questions and will perhaps (as they usually do) say rather mildly to me, "Like an egg in it?"

I say "No" pretty fast from force of habit. But on another day in another store I ask for a malted milkshake, and the clerk holds an egg in each of his hands and says:

"One or two eggs today, sir?" (Wheelerpoint 4.)

I look at the two eggs. I find it difficult to say "No" to this question, because "No" will mean nothing. He wants to know whether I want one or two, not whether or not I want any at all.

After a moment I say, "Oh, one egg will be enough!" I get the egg, the store gets 5¢ more, and the average check has gone up!

HANDLING THE DOG IN THE YARD

The vacuum cleaner man knows that dogs will run quicker for a salesman with bags in his knees and a shine in his pants. He knows, too, that words that are shiny or have bags will not help him get by the dog. Therefore, he will ask a neighbor's child the name of the dog. Armed with this information, he will open the gate cautiously, and address the dog by name, saying, "Hello, Butch, how are you today, Butch? Nice weather, isn't it, Butch? Is the lady of the house in, Butch?"

Butch, the dog, hears his name, a familiar sound to him, and perhaps says to himself: "Guess this fellow has been here before. He seems to know my name. I'll take a chance and let him on the porch."

This is a TESTED METHOD to get by a dog, and if you want to prove this to yourself, use the dog's name as you enter a yard or home with a dog in it, and watch the way his name slows up his bark!

YOUR TEN-SECOND APPEARANCE

You will quickly discover that if you dress up your words – as well as your appearance – people will respond faster and more willingly to your wishes, just as they react more favorably to a man in a dress suit than to one with his pants torn in the seat.

The vacuum cleaner man knows that if he shuffles up to the front porch and the woman sees him, she'll perhaps say to herself, "Here come another tired salesman to rest on my front porch. Watch me shoo him off fast!"

He knows, too, that there is a philosophy in pressing door

bells, and if he pushes it briskly, he will get quicker action from the woman than if he pressed it weakly like the timid beggar with the baggy pants. Women instinctively know by the ring of the doorbell just about what to expect on their front porch, just as you can tell the state of mind of the man behind you on a Sunday drive by the tone of his horn!

The seasoned door-to-door salesman knows a further rule, that of stepping to the side of the door, so that the woman finds it difficult to open the door a crack and then slam it in his face with a "Not interested!" If he stands to the side of the door jamb, the woman is forced to open the door wide to see who is on her porch, and here is where the salesman must have ready his best "Tested Selling" smile and his strongest "Tested Selling Sentence." One of the statements used by the Hoover salesman is:

"I'm here to show you how to shorten your cleaning time!"

And one beginning used by the Johns-Manville Housing Guild man, under the training of Arthur Hood, is to hand a Guild booklet to the women at the door and say:

"Here is your free copy of *101 Ways to Improve a Home!*"

These words don't have a shine on them, and they are not baggy in the knees. They are TESTED – and for that reason they work successfully in taking the stutter and stammer out of what a salesman says when the head of the prospect suddenly appears at the door.

PUT A PRESS INTO YOUR SALES LANGUAGE

The Hoover man, for instance, when he points to the light on the New Hoover, never says, "Isn't that a pretty light, madam?" There is nothing dramatic about that, so he says,

"This is our Dirt Finder. *It sees where to clean, and its clean where its been.*"

Nor does he point to the gray color of the New Hoover and say, "Isn't that a nice color – it's barnyard gray." Instead he uses the expression, "It is stratosphere gray," because the word "stratosphere" stands for speed and lightness.

Every good salesman, whether he is selling behind a counter, on a front porch, in a showroom, or over a telephone, has many three-minute sales presentations to use in bringing the brass ring around – and this prevents saturation of his prospect.

When this seasoned salesman describes anything on his sales package, he uses bright, interesting, cheerful, dramatic sales words. Then when the brass ring comes around, he has a word or two to GRAB it out of the air.

WATCH YOUR CLOSING WORDS

The Hoover man closes with: "If the Hoover goes, dirt stays; if the Hoover STAYS, dirt goes – which do you prefer?" A fine example of "Don't ask if – ask which." This Hoover close is one of many, of course, and is a hard one for a prospect to answer other than by saying she wants the cleaner to stay.

Furthermore, if the prospect offers any of the standardized objections, she will find the Hoover man well aware of the "WHY" system, and she will be confronted with a series of polite "whys" that she will find difficult to answer in words.

For instance, the salesman will say, "WHY do you want to wait until spring?" – "WHY do you feel you can't afford it?" – "WHY are you hesitating?" – "WHY do you feel you should consult your husband?"

The salesman knows this one word "why" is the HARD-EST SINGLE WORD in the English language for a person to answer, without hemming and hawing in an effort (often unsuccessful) to express himself clearly.

Try using this word "why" on people, and note the interesting and almost amusing results. And remember this secret: If somebody uses a "why" on you, come back at him with, "Why do you ask me *why?*"

A TAILOR-MADE INSURANCE STORY

Convincing people with simple selling language that has been tested to remove the guess and the gamble is too easy selling for any salesman to resort to high-pressure sales tricks, stunts, or sentences.

Sure, you can put the prospect "on the spot" with words. You can crash front doors with subterfuge – you can tell the woman you are the gas man, or a "repair man from the vacuum company," or an "inspector for the company," but once the woman discovers your REAL purpose, watch out for the rolling pin!

When a life insurance man found his prospects were constantly saying, "You can't get to first base with me, buddy," this salesman didn't come back with answers that were shiny in the seat or run down at the heel. His sales talk came fresh from the tailors, and was well pressed. It had been to the shoemaker and wasn't run down at the heel. Nor did it have on gum soles, but just plain, hard, good old leather. His tailor-made reply to these "can't-get-to-first-base-with-me" prospects was this:

"Mr. Jones, it isn't a case of whether or not I can get to first base with you, but whether your wife will get to first base with the *butcher,* the *baker,* the *candlestick maker* AFTER YOU ARE DEAD, that *really counts – isn't that true?"*

Here was a leading question even a lawyer would hesitate to answer with a "No." The salesman usually took the bite out of his prospect's "canned sales resistance" and found his sale going down the road to success because his words were measured to fit his prospects!

Remember this rule: *"Don't let your words get shiny in the seat and baggy at the knees. Keep them well-pressed and groomed."*

AVOID WORN-OUT WORDS WITH WHISKERS

There is an old codger living down the street from my house, and every time he catches me on a corner I stand there upward of fifteen minutes listening to the same worn-out expressions used by any bore.

This man will tell me something about fishing, and again and again he says, "In other words..." He then tells the story in "other words."

Why do people say, "In other words...?"

In an analysis of this in our laboratories and later out in the field of practical face-to-face contact with people, we concluded that this phrase is used by three types of people:

1. The person who fears he hasn't expressed himself properly and feels that he must keep telling you over and over again, in other words, what he has just told you.

2. The person who feels superior to you and keeps making his examples more "basic," so called, every time he sees fit to repeat himself in other words. He feels he must "talk down" to your level.

3. The person who just likes to hear himself talk, and so finds excuses to express his ideas or stories over and over again to you. He keeps the conversation in his possession, preventing you from talking, by saying, "In other words..."

If you want to be an interesting conversationalist, avoid the expression, "In other words..." Instead use Richard C. Borden's famous, "For instance..." Bring out your examples, your benefits, your proofs, by this method, or by saying, "For example... "

"LET ME MAKE MYSELF CLEARER"

Another worn-out statement with whiskers on it, and one you should cast out of your modern, streamline vocabulary is: "Let me make myself clearer..." Speak the thing properly the first time and you won't have to make it clearer. Conserve the other person's time by saying the thing *once,* so clearly that there is no need to repeat it.

It is all right to give examples, or illustrations. But to "make myself clearer" or to "make it clearer for you" not only insults the other person's intelligence, but makes you a bore.

Avoid words with whiskers! Send them to the barber!

Whenever a public speaker starts off with, "And now, ladies and gentlemen, my subject tonight will be...", he is using words with whiskers. Tell what you are going to tell. Don't tell them to prepare themselves for what you have to tell.

Avoid saying, "And now, for the next few minutes, I will discuss..."

That causes the chairs of the president's board room to shuffle and your audience to lose interest. Plunge into the topic without this self-introduction. Don't be an "And now..." person.

Here are other whiskered words for good salesmen to avoid:

"I'm tellin' you... "

"As I was saying..."

"Believe me, I told him a thing or two…"

"Can you keep this to yourself?"

"Will you keep this confidential, if I tell you..."

"Well, it was like this – I says to him..."

"I wish I had your brains..."

"You wouldn't have time for a demonstration would you?"

"My – you are an intelligent person…"

"I didn't know, *see,* otherwise I'd have gone, *see...*"

"The house was there, *you know,* and the entrance here, *you know.*"

Mr. Wilfred J. Funk, of the *Digest,* has made a list of what he considers the ten most annoying words: *Okay, lousy, terrific, contact, definitely, gal, racket, swell, impact,* and *honey.* His objection to them, he says, is that they are overworked.

WORDS THAT KILL THE SALE

Ten purchasing agents once told Mandus E. Bridston how certain words that salesmen used would kill the sale. Here are a few of these statements collected by Mr. Bridston:

"You're absolutely wrong about this!"

"Of course if you want something cheaper I can give it to you."

"I just happened to be down this way and dropped in!"

"Do you get me?"

"See?"

"Do you understand?"

"Frankly, I'd like to..."

"Frankly speaking..."

One of the purchasing agents claims that slang goes a long way, and that he would not deal with a man who used slang in lieu of speech. It seems to this buyer that all day long he has to listen to slang expressions, with one salesman actually calling him "my fran."

Another buyer condemns the salesman who sells "soft soap, but not merchandise" and is on the alert for the salesman who keeps saying, "Your pleasure is our pleasure" – "We have your interests at heart" – "A person who is as keen as you will appreciate this."

"My pet peeve," sums up a third of Mr. Bridston's purchasing agents, "is the this-is-between-you-and-me salesman. He's almost as bad as the I-wouldn't-want-this-to-get-around type, or the don't-tell-anybody-that-I-said-this type."

DON'T FLATTER OBVIOUSLY

Avoid words that bear false flattery. The prospect is on to them today. Don't gossip; if you do, the prospect knows you will gossip about him when you are with someone else.

Don't be a bore with a long string of, "I says to him..." and "He says to me..." and "See?"

Don't be an old codger with a line of, "Well, it was like this..." Give the other person a chance to do some of the talking. Be a good listener first, and a good talker second, as Professor Borden advises.

It is impossible to list the thousands of worn-out statements that people make to each other every day, that annoy people, that make you want to shout. You have to inventory your own vocabulary.

See any gray whiskers? Pluck them out.

Remember, the good rule for making people like you and for keeping you out of trouble is:

Avoid worn-out words with whiskers!

CHAPTER 20

AVOID WORDS THAT WRINKLE
THE OTHER PERSON'S BROW

There is one big lesson to be learned from the Roosevelt-Landon campaign. The days of the "Perils of Pauline" are over. Don't spoil a sale with butterfingers.

M ovie producers are changing their ideas of the average mentality of audiences. It used to be about twelve years, but now it is going upward. This means that the hokum of yesterday is no more, that the days of the "Perils of Pauline" are over, and that the hero fighting the Indian on the edge of the cliff gets laughs instead of gasps.

The fact that the American mind is growing up is not realized, unfortunately, by all copywriters, advertising people, radio people, and others who are trying to win the public to their way of thinking.

The old-fashioned preacher could frighten people into going to church on Sunday with his "Hell and brimstone." Today this doesn't succeed, as any preacher will tell you.

People like a good show. They like to hear Al Smith speak on the radio, but they only laugh when a politician talks about the country "going to the dogs." The old "dinner-pail" appeals have gone with the wind.

Many a young child tells his mother today, "You can't scare me – there's no such thing as a bogeyman." And people don't believe in Santa Claus anymore.

Little boys used to be frightened by policemen. Not today. Intelligence is banishing fears.

People are laughing today at many advertising appeals. The old medicine man has been reborn in the pages of the American press. The clever manufacturer, however, is the one who has an advertising agency that is subtle in its appeal and has the image of the medicine man buried deep behind sound logic and sensible reasoning.

Don't get me wrong: People today still buy from emotional urges, but the emotional darts that stir their instincts into action today must be "telegraphic" – not the "wooden arrows" of the Indian.

We are in a day of the "magic eye," of television, of electrical impulses flashing back and forth invisibly. So must sales language fly – invisibly!

USE "INVISIBLE" SALES WORDS

If you let the other person become CONSCIOUS he is being sold, he will wiggle the situation around with a lot of arguments that put you on the defensive.

Big words, fancy phrases, and bombastic tones are not invisible but obvious. They attract attention to you – not to what you are saying. So if you would win the other person to your way of thinking, remember this rule: *Clothe your appeals in invisible language!*

Invisible language is the *everyday language* of the masses.

If we understand quickly and readily what the other person

129

is saying without having to wrinkle our brows in thought, we are absorbing the story.

A hosiery salesgirl says to the woman who has just purchased a dollar pair of stockings in William Taylor's department store in Cleveland:

"Does one of your stockings wear out faster than the other?"

The woman naturally informs her that one stocking always gives way before the other. Seldom will runs appear simultaneously in both stockings. The clever salesgirl says:

"Then it would be advisable to buy TWO PAIRS of the SAME COLOR so that you can alternate in case one stocking tears or runs accidentally."

Simple language. No coined expressions. But on one occasion that I know of, *this store sold out a certain box of stockings that contained three pairs wrapped as a gift.*

If the young lady had said: "You can get three pairs for $2.85," the woman would say one pair was sufficient. But by using logic she cleverly induces the woman to buy the second pair, and then she says:

"If you buy the third pair, you can have it for only 85¢. You see you get *a bargain* on the third pair."

A PRESIDENT USES TESTED SELLING

The choice of words and the astute salesmanship used by President Roosevelt during the 1936 elections were classical.

Salesman Landon and Salesman Roosevelt each started out selling the same prospects. They each had about the same "product." Salesman Landon, however, had the edge on Salesman Roosevelt, because he had eighty-five percent of the newspapers and nearly all the big businessmen on his side. But Salesman Landon violated fundamental selling principles that many a door-to-door salesman would have observed instinctively.

First, he talked more about his competitor's product than about his own. He told what his competitor's product was failing to do instead of telling the benefits and advantages to be secured from his own.

Second, he called his competitor names, and he referred to his competitor by name, whereas Roosevelt usually referred to his competitor by the impersonal "they." A good salesman seldom dignifies a competitor by using his name. All competition is known to the Hoover man as a "Bojack."

Third, Salesman Landon "oversold" himself. He didn't seem to sense when to stop talking about himself and against his competitor. He talked himself quickly into a sale and then out of it.

Fourth, he used language that the public failed to comprehend and language the public knew to be trite, bombastic, and old-fashioned in the game of politics. He talked about "two chickens in every pot" and "two cars in every garage." He used the worn-out "fear campaign," with such phrases as "the country's going to the dogs" and "Roosevelt and Ruin" and "grass growing in the streets."

ROOSEVELT USED WORD MAGIC

On the other hand, Roosevelt gained the confidence of his prospect. He used language the "prospects" understood. He would say something amusing, cheerful, hopeful, and logical, such as this:

"Four years ago the White House was like an emergency hospital. Businessmen came to me with headaches and back-aches. No one knew how they suffered, except old Doc Roosevelt."

"They wanted a quick hypodermic to relieve the immediate pain, and a quick cure. I gave them both. They got action. In fact, we cured them so quickly and efficiently in Washington that now these same people are back, throwing their crutches into the doctor's face."

President Roosevelt knows the value of choosing words, of using "Tested Selling Sentences." He knows that some words sell people and others do not, and he makes certain that he uses only language tested to stamp itself on the mind of his prospect directly and instantly, and to remain there forever.

That is why the American public "bought" from him in the last election.

The rule is a simple one:

Talk in language the other person can understand without having to wrinkle his brow.

A READY-MADE RULE

The Johns-Manville man is in the neighborhood again. He is still interested in explaining Arthur Hood's new Housing Guild plan of buying home improvement on the down-payment plan, just as you purchase a refrigerator or a radio. He has planned his sales arguments, as you read some chapters before. He steps up to Mrs. Smith's front door and presses the button. When Mrs. Smith comes to the door, he gives his name and mentions the Johns-Manville Company, and then says

"This is your free copy of *101 Ways of Improving Your*

Home."

Mrs. Smith reaches for the booklet, but he turns to page 16 and says:

"This is a picture of a kitchen we just finished for your neighbor. Isn't it delightful?"

He shows her several other pictures, and then says: "Pardon me, I'm getting your home cold. I'll just step inside."

If it is summer, he says

"I seem to be letting in the flies. I'll just step inside."

HE PUTS HER AT EASE

Once inside, he puts the woman at ease by saying:

"Just sit down and make yourself comfortable, Mrs. Smith. I know you must be on your feet a great deal."

She sits down, still desiring to see more of those interesting pictures, but he wants to win her immediate liking for him, so he says:

"What lovely curtains you have. You must be an interior decorator at heart. Did you pick them out yourself?"

She is quite flattered and proceeds to explain with great pride that she picked out the curtains and, in fact, the furniture also.

Say something about the home, if you want to make your prospect like you immediately. This is a good rule for any door-to-door salesman to remember – a good rule for you to remember even when you are making a social visit..

FIVE EFFECTIVE WAYS TO MAKE
THE OTHER PERSON FEEL AT EASE

The Johns-Manville man has, on the tip of his tongue, five things he will say during the first few minutes he is with a prospect to make her feel at ease, to "break the ice," to get her interested in home improvements. He will use one or all of these five statements:

1. "Do you tire easily in the kitchen?"
2. "Are your heat and light bills high?"
3. "Is your living room too dark?"
4. "Do you enjoy games like ping-pong?"
5. "Is it difficult to keep your home warm?"

Each one of these sentences is tested to make the other person respond the way the salesman wants him to.

THE HOME IS THE FOUNDATION OF THE FAMILY

The home is the thing that is dearest to people. No matter how humble it is, it is still home. Get people discussing their home and their daydreams about dens, about larger kitchens, or about the extra room in the attic.

Here are a few more "Tested Selling Sentences" that will win people to you quickly:

"You certainly have a cheerful home."

"These rugs are very attractive. Did you pick them out yourself?"

"Any money spent on a home is well invested, isn't it?"

"If you had $300 to spend on home improvements, just what would you have done?"

"It takes more than a carpenter with a hammer to make a room as lovely as this. Was it your idea?"

When you are in the other person's home, talk about that home. You will win his affection very quickly if you follow this simple rule of putting people at ease.

THE BORDEN PRINCIPLE

Richard C. Borden, sales manager for the milk division of the Borden Company, told me how he applies "Tested Selling" on back porches to get women immediately interested in bottled malted milk. They tried many methods, sentences, and back-door stunts. The one that works best to date is to rap on the door and when the woman comes to the door to hold a bottle of the chocolate malted milk toward her and say:

"Feel how cold this is."

Once the woman has the bottle of chocolate malt in her hands, the salesman asks her to help herself to a drink. He follows her into the kitchen.

How much better this method of getting into back doors and making people TASTE your product than the old method of asking them, "Would you be interested in buying our chocolate malted milk with your regular milk?"

The driver will say something about the "lovely kitchen," and the "pretty curtains." He will use the "Rule of You" and ask:

"What is YOUR opinion of this chocolate malted milk, Mrs. Jones?"

She will tell her opinion. People like to give opinions.

If you make other people "feel at home" during the first ten seconds they are with you, you will win them over for many minutes to come.

HOW TO HANDLE IT PROPERLY

The best words, the best technique, and the best voice delivery can be spoiled if you have butterfingers and fumble what you are selling. A good salesman cultivates good hand movements. He handles the cheapest pearl necklace as if it were worth a million. His attitude toward what he is selling is important, for it reflects favorably or otherwise on the prospective owner.

Never grab hold of the item. Never fling it down on the counter. Don't take hold of it as if it were a sledge hammer or a monkey wrench. Never set the article down with a "bang," or drop it, or slide it toward the customer. Handle it with care. Create value. Operate dials, switches, and so forth, carefully, not "slam bang" but with delicacy, and so heighten the worth of what you are selling. Unfold the contract *carefully.* Hold the pen *gently.* These are small details in a sale – but important ones. *The touch counts!*

Make your movements seem simple to the prospect, so she will feel the gadget is easy to operate. Keep saying:

"This is all you have to do."
"This simply presses down."
"Doesn't this operate easily?"
"Isn't this convenient to use?"

136

GET ACTION WITH ACTION

If the prospect has been discouraged with some article and brings up the objection that it was hard to handle or operate, don't tell her this is not true. Say, "That was true of old-fashioned ones. But now see how easily these new models work."

Get the prospect to take active part in a demonstration, for this keeps up interest and prevents her mind from wandering into a field full of objections.

People like to take part. Let them. Let them operate it. Let them "run the big show." You be the master of ceremonies. Say:

"Here, try it yourself."
"See how easy it is to use."
"Doesn't this work easily?"
"You'll like using this."
"Isn't this handle comfortable?"

Desire to possess comes with handling, trying, and working the article to be purchased. Let the other person feel, smell, and taste what you are selling.

Say it with flowers!

CHAPTER 21

HOW TO MAKE TESTED SENTENCES
SELL IN DOOR-TO-DOOR SELLING

(The "Say-Something Formula")

> *The best-looking dotted line won't sign itself, as many a door-to-door salesman has discovered. And many a white-haired sales manager has discovered that the best-made product won't sell itself.*

The manufacturer can get the salesman and the product up to the door, but if the right ten-second words are not used, the salesman does not get in, and the product is not sold. Often four inches of threshold *ruin* or *make* many a product

The New York Sales Club – to which I often like to refer, as its membership of some 700 men represents a good cross section of American business executives – asked me to give a presentation of planned door-to-door selling with "Tested Selling Sentences."

Therefore I asked Mr. W. W. Powell, training director of the Hoover Company, to help me build the following serious/humorous sales skit illustrating the importance of picking words and techniques in door-to-door selling of vacuum cleaners. The presentation was given before the club on January 25, 1937.

"TESTED SELLING ON DOOR STEPS"

WHEELER: "What makes people buy in the home?

"Many of you gentlemen wonder if this 'Tested Selling' principle applies to other fields of selling, and you ask me, 'Do you believe in the "canned" sales talk?'

"Having analyzed close to 105,000 words, phrases, and selling processes and having tested them on close to 19,000,000 people, my feeling is *against* the 'canned' sales talk but in *favor* of the 'planned' sales talk.

"Today, with the help of Mr. Powell I will illustrate the difference between the so-called 'canned' sales talk and the 'planned' sales talk; and at the same time I will offer you a formula for building your own sales presentations – the 'Say-Something Formula.'

"The 'Say-Something Formula' is composed of (1) a ten-second 'attention-getter' or 'door-crasher'; (2) a three-minute sales presentation; and (3) a sixty-second close. You will find that most successful sales demonstrations are built on this simple selling formula.

"But first let us see an example of a salesman selling vacuum cleaners door-to-door, who has mechanically memorized his sales talk like a parrot. I will take the part of the salesman, and Mr. Powell will take the part first of my sales manager and then of my prospect."

SALES MANAGER POWELL: "Wheeler, here is our spring and summer sales talk on the new Bojack! Memorize it." (Gives Wheeler a large tin can.)

SALESMAN WHEELER: "Yes, Sir, Mr. Powell." (Takes tin can.)

SALES MANAGER POWELL: (Slaps Wheeler on back) "Go

to it, boy!"

WHEELER: (To audience) "Armed with my canned sales talk, I now approach my first prospect, and this is what happens to your product if it is sold with high-pressure sales language that is highly memorized."

SKIT 1
SELLING WITH A "CANNED" SALES TALK

SALESMAN: (Saunters to door. Presses the bell. Yawns. Woman answers the door.) "Good morning, madam. Is the lady of the house around? You're the maid, I take it?"

WOMAN: "Why – I'll have you understand *I'm* the lady of *this* house!"

SALESMAN: "Pardon me. I'm the salesman from the Bojack Vacuum Cleaner Company – sent here to demonstrate the New Bojack, and clean one of your *dirty* rugs."

WOMAN: "Well, now, just a minute – who told you I had a *dirty rug?"*

SALESMAN: "Well, you'd be the only family on the street that didn't! Besides, Mrs. Abernathe across the street said you certainly needed *something* to keep your house clean. I'll step in, madam. I won't take too long." (Forces himself in. The woman is dismayed but reluctantly lets him in.)

WOMAN: "I don't know who Mrs. Abernathe is, but as long as you are here – well…"

SALESMAN: "Just sit down in this chair, while I hook up this apparatus, and give your rug a good cleaning. I want you to notice in particular the beauty of this cleaner. It was designed by that fellow who designed a train or something

– I just forget his name. But this cleaner is good-looking enough to leave right here in your parlor as a permanent fixture, isn't it?"

WOMAN: "Yes, it looks all right, but speaking of parlors, my husband has two dogs. Will it remove dog hair?"

SALESMAN: (Not to be thrown off his "canned" talk.) "I'm *coming to that.* But first I want you to hear this cleaner in operation. It has a scientific humming sound that won't annoy your neighbors, and you don't want to annoy your neighbors, do you?"

WOMAN: "No, of course not, but will it remove dog hair?"

SALESMAN: "*I'm coming to that.* But first let me show you the bottom of this instrument. It's certainly a businesslike looking machine, isn't it? Why, lady, the parts in there will last longer than your rugs. In fact, this Bojack will last a lifetime, and that is what you are looking for in a cleaner, aren't you?"

WOMAN: "I really wouldn't care how long it will last, if it would remove dog hair."

SALESMAN: "Of course it will remove dog hair."

WOMAN: (Getting angry at being put off.) "But how do I know it will remove dog hair?"

SALESMAN: "*You'll have to take my word for it!* Now let me show you how it removes pieces of paper. (Throws handful of torn paper on floor.) See it pick them up? Well, almost all the pieces. That's really wonderful, isn't it?

"Madam, this cleaner is guaranteed not to rip, run, warp, tear, or stretch your most valuable rugs. Now I've cleaned one of your *dirty* rugs, and have shown you what this cleaner will do, so let's get down to the business of how much it will cost you–"

WOMAN: (Standing up and walking toward kitchen.) "I really can't give you any more time. I've a cake in the oven. Some day stop in and let me SEE if it really will remove dog hair. My present cleaner won't, and I would be interested in ANY machine that would. Goodday!"

SALESMAN: (Out on cold front porch again.) "She must have some mangy wolfhounds in her house. (Holds up tin can.) Funny there is nothing in my 'canned' sales talk about removing dog hair. If she hadn't kept throwing me off the track, I would have given a good demonstration. *She wasn't supposed to do that.* I'll have to take this up with the office!"

WHEELER: (Before audience.) "This was slightly exaggerated, to be sure, but it shows what happens to a salesman who carries his sales talk around in a can. Now let us see what happens when Salesman Powell calls on the *same* woman with a 'planned' instead of a 'canned' sales talk.

"Watch Mr. Powell's use of the 'Say-something Formula,' with his ten-second 'door-crasher' or 'attention-getter,' his three-minute sales presentation, and his sixty-second close when he finds the woman wants a cleaner that removes dog hair."

SKIT 2

SELLING WITH A "PLANNED" SALES TALK

SALESMAN: (Approaches the door briskly and in a business-like manner. Presses the bell. Removes hat. Stands back and smiles. Woman comes to door.):

"Good morning! I am Mr. Powell, the Hoover man from Gimbel's. You received a message like this, didn't you?"

142

(Shows pre-canvass literature.)

WOMAN: "Yes?"

SALESMAN: "I am calling to make good our promise to clean a whole rug and one piece of furniture free, and help *you shorten* your cleaning time. "This is our method of introducing the New Hoover Cleaning Ensemble. Gimbel's wants you to know there is no cost or obligation of any kind."

WOMAN: "A man was just here with a cleaner, and besides I have a cake in the oven."

SALESMAN: (Smiles.) *"It will only take a moment."*

WOMAN: "Well, then, step in." (The smile gets her.)

SALESMAN: (Walks in.) "I don't believe I have your name."

WOMAN: "I am Mrs. Jones."

SALESMAN: "And the initials?"

WOMAN: "Mrs. T. J. Jones."

SALESMAN: (Makes record.) "Thank you. Now just make yourself comfortable in this chair. I will take only a few minutes of your time, and I am sure you will be interested in learning how to reduce your cleaning problems." (Unfolds New Hoover.)

"This is the first basically new electric cleaner in ten years. In fact, it is a startling new development in cleaning science, for it embodies every known cleaning principle.

"It is the New Hoover 150 Cleaning Ensemble, streamlined throughout, designed by Henry Dreyfus in the manner of today, and made of magnesium, which is one-third lighter than aluminum.

"Do you see this light?"

WOMAN: "Yes."

SALESMAN: "We call it the Dirt Finder; it sees where to

clean, and it's clean where it's been.

"This red dot is the Time-to-Empty Signal."

WOMAN: "The Time-to-Empty Signal?"

SALESMAN: "Yes, the Time-to-Empty Signal. You may forget to empty the bag, but the Hoover won't.

"This is the Automatic Rug Adjuster. Just step on it. (Woman obeys.) That's all you have to do.

"This is the Instant Dusting Tool Converter. It is as easy as switching on a light." (Inserts Connector.) "That is all you have to do."

WOMAN: "That's all very interesting; but will the Hoover remove dog hair?"

SALESMAN: "Will the Hoover remove dog hair? *I'll say it will.*" (Turns Hoover over.)

"Why, Mrs. Jones, do you see these brushes? We call them the Dog Hair Removers."

WOMAN: "I never knew they had Dog Hair Removers on cleaners!"

SALESMAN: (Spreads kapok over rug.) "Now Mrs. Jones, you *see for yourself* how quickly and *easily* this kapok is removed. Kapok is similar to dog hair, only twice as hard to remove.

(Woman uses cleaner.) "You like that, don't you?"

"You see, the Hoover beats as it sweeps, as it lights, as it cleans. The Hoover gets the dirt and the dog hair you never knew you had."

(Senses woman is "sold.") "You have possibly wondered why we call this our 150 Model?"

WOMAN: "Yes, I have wondered."

SALESMAN: "Because you can have this cleaner with the Dog Hair Removers for the small sum of only one-fifty per week."

WOMAN: "Well – I don't know if my husband would approve."

SALESMAN: "One-fifty per week is only about two dimes a day. Why, you perhaps spend that much every day for knickknacks, don't you?"

WOMAN: "Come to think of it, I do."

SALESMAN: "Then I'll place my O.K. here, and just above my name *is a place for your approval;* and the problem of keeping your rugs free from dog hair will be solved! (She signs.) Thank you, Mrs. Jones."

WOMAN: (Stands, facing audience.) "Wait until I tell my husband I bought a New Hoover, and he can let the dogs back in the house!"

WHEELER: (Facing audience.) "That was certainly a fine example of scientific salesmanship. You see, gentlemen, that although the New Hoover embodies all of the newest cleaning principles which make it the first basically new cleaner in ten years, the Hoover Company realizes that these marvelous cleaning devices will pass unnoticed, or be taken as a matter of fact by women, if they are not dramatized in 'sizzle' sales language.

"Therefore, Salesman Powell used his ten-second 'doorcrasher' and got into the home, and once in the home he put on a short three-minute presentation.

"Salesman Powell followed his plan, and he made a sale without ONCE asking his prospect to 'sign on the dotted line.' Not once did he use those trite words, 'sign here,' yet the prospect signed up all right."

A STORY FROM ENGLAND

What happens when you *don't* follow a TESTED PLAN such as this? Well, it brings to mind the Hoover salesman in England who said that no good British salesman needed a "Tested Selling" plan of what to say and do. So he made up his own selling presentation. He rapped on a door and said, "Madam, I am here to show you how to cut your cleaning time in half and make life more pleasant for you."

Being a polite Englishwoman, she admitted the salesman, saying, "Any man who can make life more pleasant is always welcome!"

Inside the home he began to scatter dirt around the parlor rug, remarking, "Now, madam, the best way to show you the advantages of a Hoover is to scatter dirt about and then clean it up." The woman quite agreed. Thereupon he tore up some paper; he took a cup of flour and scattered it; he scooped up dirt in the fireplace and messed it about on the rug; and finally, he emptied all the ash trays on the floor.

He had certainly created a bad situation on the floor, but the trusting woman had confidence in his early statement that the Hoover would clean away the mess. But when he had finished making her home dirty, he said, "Now, madam, we will show you what the New Hoover will do! Where is the electric light socket?"

Whereupon the poor woman informed the salesman that unfortunately they used only gas in her home!

That's what happens when you fail to FOLLOW THE PLAN. From now on, Hoover salesmen FOLLOW THE PLAN and always place their Hoovers beside the electric light socket, immediately on entering a home, to make sure the house has electricity – before they get caught in the embarrassing situation of their good English cousin.

Always remember to follow your tested sales plan.

CHAPTER 22

HOW TO MAKE COMPLETE SALES PRESENTATIONS OUT OF TESTED SENTENCES

> *It takes only one "Tested Selling Sentence" to make a person buy. At times, however, it is necessary to put them into a series form. The difference between a "canned" and a "planned" sales talk.*

Whether you are selling something that takes ten seconds or ten days, the principles of making single sentences sell still apply.

The other person has a "fatigue" point, a limit beyond which he fails to hear what you are saying. You must revive his interest constantly by TELEGRAPHING "sizzles" to his brain. You must constantly make his mouth water for your proposition. You must always look for the "square clothespin" to crash his thoughts.

Here is a sales skit given by Warren Rishel and me at the New York Sales Executives' Club on March 29, 1937, at the Roosevelt Hotel, illustrating how single "Tested Sentences" can be coordinated chronologically into a sales presentation. Again using the principle that people learn more quickly when you first show them the wrong way and then make a sudden contrast and show them the right way, we offer you the following skit to show you how single sentences can be built into a sales presentation:

WHEELER: "Gentlemen, there are two weak links in your sales and merchandising campaigns.

"One is the selling language and techniques your salesmen will use when they face the dealer to sell your products.

"The other is the selling language and techniques the dealer will in turn use on his customers to sell your products.

"We will go back to our performance of several weeks ago to dramatize again for you the difference between the 'canned' sales talk that uses hit-and-miss salesmanship and the 'planned' sales talk that has been scientifically tested to make the sale more accurate, more foolproof, and faster.

"I will now take the part of a salesman who has overly-memorized his sales talk and otherwise violates all the rules and principles of approaching and selling a dealer on handling butter and eggs."

THE WRONG WAY TO
MAKE A SALES PRESENTATION

(Wheeler enters the store of Abernathe Schmaltz, who is busy dusting off the shelves.)

WHEELER: "Is Abernathe Schmaltz in? I take it you're the grocery boy here."

SCHMALTZ: "I'll have you understand I'm Abernathe Schmaltz."

WHEELER: "Well, howya fixed for butter and eggs in this store?"

SCHMALTZ: "Fine – wanna buy some?"

WHEELER: "Oh, you got me wrong, brother – I'm a butter-and-egg salesman. I've been sent down here to *interest* you in Bickley butter and eggs."

SCHMALTZ: "Well, go on and *interest* me!"

WHEELER: "First, I want to tell you about the background of A. F. Bickley & Sons. We've been in business since 1870, and–"

SCHMALTZ: "Well, I take butter and eggs from a farmer. Are your butter and eggs any better?"

WHEELER: "They sure are, but let me tell you about the personnel of our organization. Take our boss, for example. He's a great old duffer. Likes to fish down in Chesapeake Bay. Why you should see the fish he caught last week when he–"

SCHMALTZ: "I like fishing too, but tell me: Are your butter and eggs better than the ones I get from the farmer?"

WHEELER: "Sure they are, but let me tell you about our sales manager. He's the fellow, you know, who sent me down here to sell you. He's one of those theorists. Gets a lot of wild ideas, and us fellows out on the firing line have gotta be guinea pigs for him. Now if I was sales manager–"

SCHMALTZ: "But are your butter and eggs better than the farmer's?"

WHEELER: (Takes piece of candy out of box.) "Sure they're better, but–"

SCHMALTZ: "Say, don't eat that piece of candy – that's MY PROFITS!"

WHEELER: "Sorry – but now look-it here, Schmaltz, we're wasting a lot of time. I want to do you one favor."

SCHMALTZ: (Angry.) "Oh, you want to do me a favor, heh?"

WHEELER: "I sure do. Now if you–"

SCHMALTZ: "Then git the blazes out of this store! That's the biggest favor *you* can do for me. I've lost $2.85 in sales already. Now git, you – darn you, git!"

WHEELER: "Gee, these grocery fellows are certainly hard people to sell. Guess it's account of that Patman Bill."

THE RIGHT WAY TO
MAKE A SALES PRESENTATION

WHEELER: (To audience.) "That was slightly exaggerated, to be sure, but it illustrates a mighty important principle in selling today, which is this:

"A salesman calling on a dealer has only ten short seconds to catch the dealer's interest, and if in those ten short seconds he doesn't say something mighty important, the dealer will leave him, either physically or mentally.

"Now let us see this same salesman one month later, after he has thrown away his 'canned' sales talk and has made a careful study of the 'planned' TESTED presentation style of selling.

"Not only does he now have ten-second door-crashers, 'Tested Selling Sentences,' and 'Tested Techniques,' but he also has an interesting plan of giving the dealer ready-made words and sales techniques to help the dealer build his volume.

"I'll again take the role of the salesman."

(Wheeler enters store in breezy manner.)

WHEELER: "Good morning, Mr. Schmaltz, my name is Wheeler. I'm from A. F. Bickley & Sons. *How would you like to build your butter-and-egg business?*"

SCHMALTZ: "Guess I would. Who wouldn't?"

WHEELER: "Feel the weight of this egg." (Puts eggs into Schmaltz's right hand.) "Now feel the weight of this egg!" (Puts another egg into Schmaltz's left hand.) "The egg in your right hand is much heavier than the egg in your left hand, yet both eggs are the same size. Isn't that true?"

SCHMALTZ: (Puzzled.) "Yes this egg is heavier – how come?"

WHEELER: "That is a Bickley farm-controlled egg, Mr. Schmaltz, laid by a hen that has been fed scientifically balanced food that contains calcium."

SCHMALTZ: "Calcium? What is calcium?"

WHEELER: "Calcium is the bone – and body – building food in an egg.

"The more calcium and other food in an egg, the *heavier* it is.

"The *outside* of an egg is no indication of the inside.

"Whether the egg is brown or white is no way to determine the food value inside the shell.

"You must weigh eggs to determine the amount of food value in them. Good eggs should weigh no less than 24 ounces a dozen.

"The hen who laid that egg in your left hand was fed on run-of-the-farm left-overs. It has little food. That is why it feels so light.

"The egg in your right hand is the same size and same color, yet weighs much more. It is a Bickley farm-controlled egg. It is filled with body-building calcium."

SCHMALTZ: "My, I never knew that."

WHEELER: "And I'll bet few of your customers know this interesting story of eggs. They merely buy eggs by color and price. But if you took ten short seconds to tell them this Bickley calcium story, you'd sell more higher-priced eggs, wouldn't you?"

SCHMALTZ: "Guess I would. Calcium farm-controlled eggs sound good to me." (As he is thinking out loud, a customer enters.)

CUSTOMER ONE: "I want some pepper."

SCHMALTZ: "Five – or ten-cent size?"

CUSTOMER ONE: "Oh, the five-cent size will be all right."

SCHMALTZ: "How about some sardines today?"

CUSTOMER ONE: "No, just the five-cent pepper, please." (Customer leaves.)

WHEELER: "How would you like to sell your customers large sizes instead of small sizes?"

SCHMALTZ: (Interested.) "Sure I would. Got some more of them magic words for pepper?"

WHEELER: "Yes. The next time a customer asks for anything that comes in two sizes, don't suggest the small size, but use this 'sizzle': Say, 'The family size?' Or 'The economical size?'

SCHMALTZ: "'The family size?' 'The economical size?'"

WHEELER: "Now if you want to sell sardines, as a suggested extra sale, place a box down in front of the woman and say: 'These sardines are turned *upside down every month.*'
"When the woman asks why, tell her that this allows the olive oil to seep through the sardines so that they won't dry out in the can."

SCHMALTZ: "Say, those are swell merchandising ideas! Here comes a customer. Watch me try these 'sizzles' on her."

CUSTOMER TWO: "I want some Rinso."

SCHMALTZ: "The economical family size, Mrs. Perkins?"

CUSTOMER TWO: "Oh, of course."

SCHMALTZ: (Gives her the Rinso, and then holds sardines in front of her.) "These sardines are turned *upside down every month,* Mrs. Perkins."

CUSTOMER TWO: (Surprised and interested.) "Turned upside down every month? My, what for?"

SCHMALTZ: "So that the olive oil can seep through the little sardines and keep them from drying up. *They'll taste better.*"

CUSTOMER TWO: "That is an idea, and I'll bet those sardines do taste good. I'll take a can."

SCHMALTZ: "The economical family size?"

CUSTOMER TWO: "Oh, yes, I always buy *economically.*" (Gets package and leaves store.)

SCHMALTZ: (Delighted.) "It worked, young man! That's the first time old lady Perkins ever bought the large Size package of soap, and lordy, I've never sold her twenty-five-cent sardines since just before the depression!"

WHEELER: "That's a practical example of what 'Tested Techniques' and 'Tested Selling Sentences,' or magic words, as you call them, really do in making people buy.

"Mr. Schmaltz, *which* do you sell the most of, the white or the brown eggs?"

SCHMALTZ: "Oh, I sell nearly all white eggs in this community."

WHEELER: *"When* would you like me to send you a box of our white calcium eggs, on *Monday* or *Tuesday?"*

SCHMALTZ: (Absent-mindedly.) "Monday will be all right."

WHEELER: "Good-day. I'll send this order out promptly C.O.D., and I'll be back next week with some more 'Tested Selling Sentences' to help you build your business."

SCHMALTZ: (Suddenly comes out of daze.) "Say – say you, young feller – too late – he's gone, and I bought some eggs from that feller, and I really didn't need them till next week. He musta used some of that magic on me. But pshaw! He's a nice fellow."

CHAPTER 23

HOW TO SELL THE MAN SHOPPING
FOR HIS WIFE OR SWEETHEART

(From a Talk by Mr. Wheeler before R. H. Macy & Co.)

> *So much scientific data has been brought to light these past few years showing that women do 85 percent of the buying that the art and science of selling the humble male is being lost or taken as a matter of fact.*

It is a well-known fact in retail stores that when a humble male comes into the ladies' department, he is shown the best-priced lines at once – for he is a quick buyer. Price is a secondary thought. He is embarrassed. He wants to make a fast purchase and leave quickly.

If he sees only the expensive merchandise, he makes up his mind on which of the higher-priced items he wants, pays, and goes out.

Women, on the other hand, are "shoppers." They make the salesperson show item after item, and they keep looking until they get the best bargains. They are bargain hunters.

Recently R. H. Macy & Company became "word-conscious," realizing that the finest merchandise won't sell itself, no matter how attractive it is; that greater sales always result when the salesperson uses persuasive language and techniques.

I was asked to address first a group of 200 buyers and merchandising officials and then, at a later meeting, many of the 12,000 employees of this world-important organization.

After chatting with Mr. Paul Hollister, vice president of the store, it was decided that the salespeople would catch the idea of properly choosing their words and selling techniques through presentations. It was agreed that first they must be shown, in a dramatized manner, the wrong way to make a sale, and immediately afterwards the right way. The sudden contrast would prove a good bit of instruction.

Therefore the following two skits were presented. They are slightly exaggerated for theatrical purposes, but withal they carry their selling points well and illustrate the five Wheeler-points:

1. "Don't Sell the Steak – Sell the Sizzle!"
2. "Don't Write – Telegraph!"
3. "Say It With Flowers!"
4. "Don't Ask If – Ask WHICH!"
5. "Watch Your Bark!"

SELLING DEMONSTRATION I

The Wrong Way to Sell Powder and Perfume To a Man Shopping for His Wife

CLERK: (Powdering nose.) "I'll be with you in a minute."
CUSTOMER: "Do you sell powder here?"
CLERK: "Yes, we do."
CUSTOMER: "Well, I'd like to buy some."
CLERK: (Looking strangely at customer.) "Yes, what shade do you wear?"

CUSTOMER: "It's not for me; it's for my wife."

CLERK: "Is she blonde or brunette?"

CUSTOMER: "She's a redhead."

CLERK: "Well, here's something good for her."

CUSTOMER: "How much?"

CLERK: "Let's see." (Looks at label on box.) "It's $1.50."

CUSTOMER: "Oh that's too much money. Do you have any- thing cheaper?"

CLERK: "Here is another one at $1.00 that's pretty good."

CUSTOMER: "Well, what is the *difference* between the $1.00 and $1.50 box?"

CLERK: "Between you and me the color on the box is the only difference. All us girls use the red dollar box." (Gets confidential with customer.)

CUSTOMER: "Humph! Give me the dollar box then."

CLERK: *"How are ya fixed for perfume?"*

CUSTOMER: "No, thanks, I never use it."

CLERK: "Not for you; for your wife – the redheaded one!"

CUSTOMER: "No, that will be all; I'm in a hurry."

CLERK: "But it's so cheap."

CUSTOMER: "No, not today."

CLERK: "But it's only $5.00."

CUSTOMER: "No – JUST powder!"

CLERK: "But we've got a contest on today, and"

CUSTOMER: (Getting angry.) "I don't care about your con- tests. I'll be back some other time." (Hurrying out of store.)

"Such high pressure. I'll never come back again.

CLERK: "People haven't got any money these days."

The Right Way to Sell Powder and Perfume
To a Man Shopping for His Wife

CLERK: "Lovely morning, isn't it?"

CUSTOMER: "Yes, it is... I'd like to see some powder."

CLERK: "Did you want it for a blonde or a brunette?"

CUSTOMER: "A redhead."

CLERK: "Here is something that is very becoming to redheads."

CUSTOMER: "How much is it?"

CLERK: "It's $1.50."

CUSTOMER: "That's quite a bit; got anything cheaper?"

CLERK: "Yes, Sir, here's some at $1.00."

CUSTOMER: "What is the *difference* between the $1.00 and $1.50 powder?"

CLERK: "The $1.50 powder is made *especially* for redheads, and will cling to the skin longer.

"She won't have to powder so often. *It's very lasting!*"

CUSTOMER: "Clings to skin longer... very lasting... that's fine!" (To himself)

"Maybe I won't see her using her puff everywhere I take her."

CLERK: (Smells perfume. Offers it to customer.) "Doesn't this perfume have a lovely fragrance?"

CUSTOMER: "Yes, it has. What is it?"

CLERK: "This is Mitzy Perfume; it has a spicy fragrance *especially* made for redheads – and it is very LASTING."

CUSTOMER: "That lasting, too? Then she won't have to use as much!"

CLERK: "It will *save* you money."

CUSTOMER: "I'll take that too. I like your store. It tells me how to save money."

CLERK: "Perhaps you'd like to get a bottle for your mother for Mother's Day?"

CUSTOMER: (Very sad.) "I don't have a mother."

CLERK: (Coquettishly.) "Isn't there *someone* else?"

CUSTOMER: (Sheepishly.) "Someone *else?* Let me see..." (Laughter.)

As mentioned, these skits are simple, yet they have proved highly effective when acted properly. They carry a sermon with every laugh. The salesperson sees herself as others see her and realizes that a sales presentation after all is a series of single "Tested Sentences."

Let us see the second skit now.

SELLING DEMONSTRATION 2

The Wrong Way to Sell a Man Hose for His Wife

CLERK: (Standing by, yawning.) "Are you bein' waited on?"

CUSTOMER: "My wife said to me this morning, 'Charlie, buy me some hose on the way home.' Do you sell hose here?"

CLERK: "Sure we do."

CUSTOMER: "Can I look at some?"

CLERK: "Sure – what size does your wife take?"

CUSTOMER: "Why, she didn't say."

CLERK: "Well, how long have you been married?"

CUSTOMER: "Thirteen years, why?"

CLERK: "Then you ought to know what size hose your wife wears. Put your foot on the counter." (Customer places foot on counter.)

CLERK: "Is her foot as large as yours?"

CUSTOMER: "No – only about half."

CLERK: "Then she'll take size 10. Now, here's a swell pair at $1.50."

CUSTOMER: "Haven't you anything cheaper?"

CLERK: "Sure, here's some at a dollar."

CUSTOMER: "What's the difference?"

CLERK: "Fifty cents *difference;* but all us girls wear the $1.00 ones, and we like them."

CUSTOMER: "Hump – well, give me the $1.00 pair. If they're good enough for you clerks, they're good enough for my wife."

CLERK: "How about two pair?"

CUSTOMER: "No, my wife only wears one pair at a time."

CLERK: "Well, why not be generous and buy her two pair?"

CUSTOMER: "Nope – just one. Hurry."

CLERK: "But my sales book is low today and I need some sales..." (Follows customer off stage, trying to sell him.)

CUSTOMER: "I'll be back some other time. The dumb clerks the way they high pressure you today!"

CLERK: "The dumb customers. They don't have any money in their pockets these days."

The Right Way to Sell a Man Hose for His Wife

CLERK: "Good morning."

CUSTOMER: "Good morning." (Looks at hose on counter.)

CLERK: "They are lovely hose, aren't they?"

CUSTOMER: "Yes, my wife asked me to buy her a pair."

CLERK: "What size stocking does your wife wear, sir?"

CUSTOMER: "Oh! She forgot to tell me."

CLERK: "Then I'll give you 9½; that's the average size. Here is a very fine pair."

CUSTOMER: "How much are they?"

CLERK: "They are $1.50."

CUSTOMER: "Hmm, do you have anything cheaper?"

CLERK: "Yes, sir, these are $1.00."

CUSTOMER: "What is the *difference* between the $1.00 and $1.50 hose?"

CLERK: "The $1.50 hose will give your wife MORE MILES of service!"

CUSTOMER: *More miles of service!* Well, that's what she needs; she's always walking them out. I'll take a pair."

CLERK: "Does one of your wife's stockings wear out *before* the other?"

CUSTOMER: "Indeed it does. She's always tearing one and throwing the other away."

CLERK: "Wouldn't it be GOOD BUSINESS to buy two pair of the same color, so she can *alternate* if one stocking tears or runs?"

CUSTOMER: "Say, that is good business! I'll take two pair."

CLERK: "You can now have the third pair for only $1.25. You save twenty-five cents, the price of two good cigars.

CUSTOMER: "I'll take three pair – anything to save money." (Leaving store.) "Nice salespeople in this store. They are really helpful."

CLERK: "The customers certainly are spending more money these days!"

You must use words to train the other person in how to sell, as well as to train yourself in what to say and do. You will find the other person will learn more quickly and with greater ease if you show first the wrong way of making a given sale and then the right way.

Since these skits were presented at Macy's, they have been given before several retail groups elsewhere, and the results have always been the same – the salespeople went away from each meeting laughing, yet with a much keener idea of the value their words and selling methods have in making people buy.

Remember the principle:

A sales presentation is nothing more than a series of "Tested Sentences" arranged in chronological order.

CHAPTER 24

A LESSON IN SALESMANSHIP
AT THE SEASHORE

Selling is like fishing. You must bait your hook with the food the prospect likes. Joseph Day sells Carnegie a building.

Fluke are fish caught in salt water, and they are quite abundant around Long Island. I like to fish for fluke. It is an interesting sport at times, although fluke are lazy fish. They are thin and wide. Some people call them "door mats." They are white on the bottom and dark on the top. This is for protection. The dark top is invisible from above the fish.

The fluke swims close to the bottom of the sea. It is easygoing and is influenced by the tides. When the tide begins to flow, the fluke is stirred up, permits itself to move in the direction of the tide.

To catch the fluke, you attach a live killie, a small fish about two or three times the size of a minnow, by its tail to a hook with a three-foot leader and a sinker that takes the killie down close to the bottom of the sea. The killie swims around trying to get away from the hook that is holding it by its tail. The fluke opens its mouth, takes the killie's head, and holds it for several minutes. The fisherman doesn't realize this.

After a while the fisherman becomes restless and begins moving the line up and down, and the killie begins to slide out of the fluke's mouth. The fluke is evidently warned that it is going to lose the killie and so he takes the killie *entirely* into its mouth.

HOOKING THE FLUKE

If the fisherman stops moving the line, the fluke continues to hold the killie in its mouth, but if the fisherman again moves the line, the fluke becomes fearful of losing the nice morsel and swallows the killie entirely. He is then hooked.

Now the experienced fisherman knows this eating habit of the fluke. He raises his anchor and allows his boat to drift with the tide, so that the killie is drifting on the sea bottom when it comes upon a lazy fluke. The fluke takes hold of the killie's head, immediately feels the killie start drifting away, and, fearing he will lose his bait, swallows it and is hooked.

Therefore, if you want to catch fluke, keep the line moving up and down. Drift with the tide and you will float by the lazy fluke. On the other hand, if you let the bait alone, the fluke will merely hold onto the killie, and perhaps decide to release it.

SAME PRINCIPLE IN SELLING

How true this principle is in selling an idea to your friends or your business associates, or in selling anybody anything. Let them feel you are overly anxious, let them feel the supply is unlimited, and they will postpone buying. But let them taste what you have to offer, then start pulling the bait away from them, and watch certain types of people make a lunge and get caught in your sales trap.

There comes a time in many a negotiation when it is advisable to remove the offer, explaining that the time limit is up and you must offer it elsewhere. This is the point where many people will buy – quickly.

If you let a prospect feel that two other people are bidding for your services, his interest will be aroused. People want what other people want. It is a human trait.

THE GREGARIOUS INSTINCT

We love crowds. We like to bump elbows with people. It is the mass urge in human beings. It is called the "gregarious instinct." Sheep huddle together. Other animals huddle together. People go into restaurants that are crowded. They like stores with small aisles that fill up quickly. Many stores *deliberately* have small aisles and tiny elevators. People feel that the store is selling good merchandise if many people are in the store.

Remember the story of the fluke. Remember that your prospects are lazy on the whole and will not "take you up" until you begin to tug the bait tactfully, making it jump up and down, or threaten to remove it entirely.

Be on the alert for the "fluke type of buyer." When you find him, handle him with the "fluke method." If you find a "trout buyer," sell him on the fly.

Withal, don't forget the rule: Catch the prospect or the fish with the kind of bait *he* likes, and not with what you like.

"You" is a greater money-securing word than "I."

ANOTHER FISH STORY

A few weeks ago I took my fishing pole and called on an old friend of mine, J. A. Greulich, who spends considerable time fishing. We went to a new fishing station to try our luck. On approaching the station to buy our bait, Jay asked the attendant how the fish were biting.

"Fine," said the fisherman.

"What kind of bait do you sell?"

"What kind of bait do you like?" replied the attendant. "We have all kinds."

"Well," said Jay, "it isn't what I like, *but what the fish like.* Tell me, what are the fish biting on in these waters?"

The attendant told him sand worms, so we bought some and caught a nice mess of fish.

Now that incident, which was humorous to start with, gradually took on a new light to me as the day went on. I fashioned out this rule: Catch fish with the bait *they* like, not the bait *you* like. In other words, I like a good juicy steak, but the fish would not bite on steak. They want what *they* like.

In selling, this same rule applies. Use the bait that the prospect will like. That is why many salesmen find out in advance the likes and dislikes of a prospect. If he is a rabid football fan, then familiarize yourself with some football technique. But if he detests football games, never, NEVER talk about football games.

Every housewife knows this rule of winning and holding the man through his stomach, and she feeds him the food he likes.

JOSEPH DAY MAKES A SALE

Joseph Day, New York's foremost realtor, was sitting in the Empire Building in lower New York, discussing new offices with Elbert Gary. Day wanted to change Gary's mind *without* resentment. Gary wanted to move into better offices to oblige the young directors who were coming into the company.

According to E. T. Webb and J. P. Morgan, in their book, *Strategy in Handling People,* this is the way Day changed Gary's mind:

"Judge, where was your office when you first came to New York?"

"Why, it was in this building," replied Gary.

After a short pause Day asked, "Judge, where was the Steel Corporation formed?"

"Right here in this very room."

Day let these two single selling sentences sink into Gary's mind. In a few seconds they struck home, and Gary exclaimed, "We were born here – we've grown up here – and *here* is where we are going to stay!"

The art of changing the other person's mind without resentment is to let him change it himself, by laying certain facts, tactfully, before him and letting him munch on them.

Mr. Paul Lewis, associated with me, told me of his neighbor up in Riverdale, Connecticut, who catches fish on rainy days, sunny days, cloudy days; on winter, spring, fall, summer days. He immediately cuts them open. He sees what kind of food the fish have eaten that day. *He then knows what bait to use to catch the fish.*

Of course we can't dissect the prospect, but we can find out what is on his mind, what kind of "mental food" he likes, and then feed him *his own* food.

I may like spaghetti, but I would not fish with spaghetti if I wanted to catch fish. I'd use the bait the fish liked. If I took a client to dinner, I would not order for him the food I liked, but the food *he* liked.

How do you find out the "mental dishes" he likes? By inquiring before you attack! By asking questions – by being a "question-mark" and not an "exclamation-point" interviewer.

Lord Chesterfield once said: "By observing his favorite topic of conversation, you will discover a man's prevailing vanity."

Let the other fellow do 99 percent of the talking. Learn by listening!

That is the way to find out what is on his mind; and once you have this information, feed him the "mental dishes" he likes.

The rule is simple:

**"Feed him the bait he likes –
and you will sell him!"**

CHAPTER 25

THE WORD "MISS" VERSUS
THE WORD "MRS."

(Tested Selling Over Telephones)

> *One little word that was worth a thousand dollars.*
> *The voice with the smile wins over the telephone.*
> *Handling the maid. Your first ten telephone words*
> *are more important than your next ten thousand.*

The Charles Mitchells, father and son, are owners of the Regal Laundry in Baltimore and members of the Baltimore Advertising Club. I had talked before this group and inspired Charles Mitchell, Jr., to ask that a survey be made of the sales language employed by his telephone operators and drivers.

The Regal Laundry, being very progressive, had a monitor system that permitted an observer to "cut in" on a telephone conversation between the Regal telephone solicitors and the prospects. After a mass of data was collected, it was noted that the married women were getting more orders than the single girls. Over the telephone a voice is a voice, and it is difficult to discern between the voice of a married woman and that of a single woman. What, then, was causing the married solicitors to get more business? Was it the famous "voice with the smile"? This circumstance had us perplexed for several weeks, and then we made this interesting observation.

170

WOMEN WON'T HANG UP ON A "MRS."

It seems that if you call a prospect and say, "This is *Mrs.* Smith of the Regal Laundry calling," the prospect on the other end of the telephone hesitates to hang up. She feels that a married woman deserves consideration, for she is married herself! Besides, what could a single woman tell her about her washing problems?

As an experiment, we instructed the entire telephone staff to begin using the word "Mrs." affixed to their names, instead of "Miss." People began to listen to the Regal sales story!

This one word has meant thousands of dollars in extra business.

WHEN THE MAID ANSWERS

Often the maid will answer the telephone. In this case the Regal solicitor is instructed to say very simply: *"Please tell Mrs. Jones that Mrs. Smith is calling."* Again the "Mrs." works magic.

When the mistress answers the telephone, the solicitor will get her immediate attention with this:

"I am calling about your laundry and dry cleaning." What woman can hang up on this harmless statement?

Few did.

The next step was to find where and how this prospect had her laundry done each week, in order to know what sales appeals to use in the solicitation. The statement that secured this information was this:

"Do you send your laundry out, Mrs. Jones, or is it done at home?"

Regardless of the reply, the Regal salesgirl had an opportunity to explain the benefits that would be derived if the woman would allow Regal to do her work.

Selling is so simple – why complicate it?

OVERCOMING OBJECTIONS

How many objections do you believe a woman could give a laundry sales solicitor? Well, there are forty resistances – forty objections. Here are a few:

I do my own washing.
Laundries are hard on clothes.
Laundries lose things.
Laundries keep clothes too long.
I have a maid.
I am satisfied with my present laundry.
You laundries wash my clothing with other people's.
The Chinaman is cheaper.

All of these objections have a logical reply, and always in front of the telephone solicitors are these forty objections – and their "Tested Answers." Selling services on back porches or over telephones or across counters has the same basic principles of using good sales language.

A good rule to practice is: *Learn the other fellow's objections beforehand, and have your replies ready-made!*

A FEW EXAMPLES

Here are a few "Tested Answers" to laundry objections:

OBJECTION: Laundry companies lose things.

ANSWER: Regal uses the new four-way checking system employed in the United States mail offices.

OBJECTION: Laundries wash my clothing with other people's.

ANSWER: Regal places your laundry in INDIVIDUAL PULLMAN TUBS, and it never comes in contact with any-one else's laundry.

OBJECTION: Laundries are hard on clothes.

ANSWER: We use Palmolive Soap Beads in soft water, which is more gentle to your clothes than the ordinary hard faucet water at home.

There is always an answer to every sales objection, and if you will sit down quietly by yourself and tabulate all of the res-istances you feel the other person will give you, and then devise the ready-made answers you will use, you will find that the sale will begin for you with the first objection.

So a good sales motto to follow is this: *Get the resistances in advance; then prepare the answers you will use and have them on the tip of your tongue for ready use at the first sign of the objection.*

THE MAN AT YOUR BACK DOOR

The man who calls at your back door to interest you in his laundry, milk, bread, or any other service is aware of the Rule of Ten Seconds. He is allowed ten seconds to tell you who he is and the purpose of his call.

One effective Regal Laundry approach was to rap on the back door and, holding a man's freshly laundered shirt in full view, say to the woman when she responded:

"This is a sample of the way the Regal Laundry is cleaning shirts for many husbands in this neighborhood."

The salesman immediately reverts to the question-mark principle to qualify his prospect, and says:

"Do you launder your husband's shirts or send them out?"

She tells him, and regardless of the reply, the sale is on its merry way. (Wheelerpoint 4, "Don't Ask If – Ask Which!")

You must watch those first ten seconds – your first ten words. The point always to remember is this:

**You first ten words are more important
than your next ten thousand.**

CHAPTER 26

"OLD MAN JOHNSTON" FINDS SIX WORDS THAT SELL PIPE TOBACCO

> *This is the story of a man who took fifty years to find a "Tested Selling Sentence" with sufficient "sizzle" to overcome a typical customer objection. He makes six words sell hundreds of pounds of pipe tobacco.*

For fifty years, C. E. Johnston, tobacco blender of Cleveland, Ohio, worked for a leading tobacconist. One morning he was fired. "Old Man Johnston" was let out because he was thought too old to carry on.

But with grim determination to carry on he began selling electrical devices of all kinds door to door. But the devices had no "repeat value." They were "one-time" sales. Mr. Johnston couldn't build up a trade – a following.

He began to sell other gadgets; then suddenly he decided to capitalize on his fifty years as a tobacco blender. A natural thing to do – such an obvious thing – yet it had taken him fifty years to think of the idea. He invested in $22.00 worth of Irish tobaccos. He blended them to a taste he felt would please a great number of particular pipe smokers.

"YOUR TOBACCO IS TOO EXPENSIVE"

He used only good tobaccos, and since good tobaccos are

expensive, they must bring a fair price. So he charged $3.00 a pound. Naturally he had a price resistance, the same one he had heard for fifty years in his former place of business. People would say to him, "Your tobacco is good, Mr. Johnston, but it is too expensive for me to smoke regularly."

With this objection facing him wherever he went, Mr. Johnston was quite discouraged. It took him 42 days, he told me, to sell his first order of Irish tobacco.

One day he hit upon an answer to the objection. He tried it out. It clicked. It began to convince people that his tobacco was not expensive – but really cheap.

SIX SIMPLE SALES WORDS

How did he accomplish this? With six simple sales words, tested to make people buy his tobacco. Here is how he did it: He would listen to the old objection and then ask the prospect for a cigarette. He would hold the cigarette in his hand, dramatically (Saying it With Flowers). He would then say:

"Did you know cigarettes cost you $9.00 a pound?"

The prospect gasped! "What? Nine dollars a pound!" "Sure – figure it out for yourself! Cigarettes do cost that much per pound, but who realizes it?"

The prospect saw how cheap pipe tobacco was – even the most expensive pipe tobacco – when this "Tested Selling Sentence" was hurled at him, and he came to a sudden realization that Mr. Johnston's fine Irish blends, at $3.00 a pound, cost $6.00 a pound *less* than cigarettes.

THIS TESTED SENTENCE
GETS 1600 CUSTOMERS

During the past three years Mr. Johnston has built up a following of nearly 1600 businessmen of Cleveland. All of them know Mr. Johnston. He is welcome in all their offices.

Those six well-thought-out words, fifty years in the making, have sold hundreds of pounds of tobacco for Mr. Johnston. Sometime try his Number 12 tobacco. You'll like it and you'll like a man who, at seventy years, found that you are never too old to learn the rule:

"Consider the prospect's
response to what you say."

CHAPTER 27

SELLING-SENTENCE ODDITIES THAT
HAVE MADE PEOPLE RESPOND

Oddities in selling have their place. But "tricky" door-openers and attention-getters harm sales. Use the odd only when it is dignified and moves the sale smoothly toward a close. The book salesman's approach. When you find the sign, "No Canvassers Allowed."

I have always been interested in the science of "door crashing," the great American art of getting inside the home of a busy housewife with a cake in the oven and two children to dress for school.

Perhaps one of the most amusing door crashers that has come to my attention recently, as used by a salesman for one of those educational schoolbooks, goes as follows:

SALESMAN: (Rapping on door.) "Do you have a little girl named Dorothy?"

WOMAN: (Wondering.) "Oh, no, I have a boy named Harold."

SALESMAN: "Oh, yes, Harold is the name. He is backward in his history, isn't he?"

WOMAN: "Well, I didn't know. I thought it was writing."

SALESMAN: "I would like to show you how Harold can get

better marks in his writing at school. May I step in? It will take only a moment."

WOMAN: (Wiping her hands on her apron.) "Oh, certainly, do come in."

It is often the simple things that make people respond. Things so simple any of us could have thought them up, but so original that none of us ever has. However, BEWARE. Don't use tricks to get to the prospect, because when she discovers your deceptive tricks, beware of her rolling pin!

"IF YOU RUN A LITTLE"

One tailor uses this sentence on his store, and it works: "Pants Pressed – 10¢ a leg!"

Ridiculous? Sure. But he says it in a split second. He telegraphs his message.

When a prospect refuses to come to the back door, one door-to-door salesman I know of goes to the front door and says:

"I didn't think you were receiving at the back door today, so I called at the front door."

Improbable? Perhaps. But it works for him.

One real estate salesman gets away with this light banter. He always tells the prospect, with a smile, of course, "Now this fine house is only five minutes from the Long Island Railroad – *if you run a little.*"

Another real estate man I know has often told me: "If the place has an eight-foot closet, I'll sell the entire house."

The management of a department store in New York told its piano buyer one day, so I am informed, that he couldn't allow people to take eighteen months to pay, because that tied up its money too long. The management stated that the department could allow piano purchasers only twelve months to pay, instead of the usual eighteen months. Everywhere else in New York people could still purchase on the eighteen-month plan. After some thought, the buyer, not be discouraged, ran full-page advertisements shouting:

"A Whole Year to Pay!"

People read the advertisement. "A whole year to pay?" they would say. "That is certainly considerate of the store." Sales increased! This was taking a handicap and turning it into a selling "sizzle."

Don't sell the piano – sell a whole year to pay for it! Even pianos have "sizzles."

"NO CANVASSERS ALLOWED"

W. W. Powell, of the Hoover Company, sold 92 percent of the people who had signs on their doors saying: "No Canvassers or Beggars Allowed."

When I asked him what his reasoning was, he told me that only people with weak sales resistance put up those signs, *after* they had bought *so much* from front-porch salesmen that they secured the sign for self-protection.

Zenn Kaufman, who with Ken Goode wrote, *Showmanship in Business,* tells how the Electrolux salesman "Says It with Flowers" by lighting a giant size match, saying, "It runs as silently as this match burns!"

One of New York City's foremost department stores saved

itself nearly $7,000 in unnecessary delivery costs by giving its clerks "Tested Selling Sentences" which we had designed to induce customers to carry their own small packages.

For instance, when a small boy finished purchasing a new suit with his mother, the clerk would say to the boy, "Would you like to wear this suit tonight?" The boy would usually reply, "Sure." Mother would say, "Then you'll have to carry the package yourself, Son, as Mother's arms are full."

"Are you in the open much?" proved an attention-getter in three New York department stores during our recent tests for Pro-Phy-Lac-Tic Brush Company to find best sentences and techniques to use in selling their Stranzit hair brush.

"Does your brush have these wave-like bristles?" proved another sales-getter, and the sentence, "Do you strand your hair while brushing?" doubled sales of this brush in Lord & Taylor's and Gimbel's of New York in three days' time!

THE MOVING VAN BUSINESS

Mr. Buell Miller, vice president of the Mayflower Ware-housemen's Association, made up of leading moving companies of the nation, employed our services to help his estimators say and do the right thing when quoting prices for moving.

This research is new to us as this book goes to press, and our findings for this industry are not all catalogued, but one "sizzle" that seems to be going over very well is to have the estimator show his appreciation of fine things by picking out a piece of furniture he believes is cherished by the woman and saying: "That is a very fine piece, isn't it?"

The woman sees the estimator knows good furniture, and she has the peace of mind necessary before she gives the order.

This one selling principle is helping to remove the nightmare from moving by giving the customer confidence.

When the drivers arrive to begin moving, they are instructed to wash their hands in the kitchen sink or basement, saying: "We are instructed to wash our hands before touching your furniture." Again one sentence goes a long way toward building confidence for this moving association, and is securing business through giving customers peace of mind.

"STOP, LOOK, LISTEN"

Did you ever realize that the following three commonly seen statements are "Tested Selling Sentences," sentences that were created to make people respond?

"No down payment."
"Send no money."
"Free sample."

We see these expressions so *much* that we don't realize they are "selling sentences," and tested ones, at that.

I am told that since they changed the reading on the weighing machines in the subways of New York from "Insert one cent" to "Insert coin," out of every 100 coins now received several are nickels and a few dimes! Besides that, more coins are found! People who had five-cent pieces and wanted to be weighed were afraid they would injure the machine or would not get weighed if they inserted coins other than pennies. When the inscription merely said "Insert coin," well, that could mean a five-cent or a ten-cent piece, as well as the usual penny.

THE REDHEADED BOY

I am told that when a young fellow applying for a job found a long line of boys ahead of him, he immediately went to the telegraph office and sent a telegram saying:

"BEFORE HIRING ANYONE SEE REDHEADED BOY AT END OF LINE."

He didn't write – he telegraphed, in all senses of the word!

"Servicing" the mechanical purchase is better than "repairing" it. So "Service Departments" have come to take the place of "Repair Departments."

"Beware of Hungry Dogs" is more effective in front of farm houses than "Beware of Dogs."

Here are some other popular expressions we don't realize are time-tested sales words that make people respond:

"Safety first."
"No cash needed."
"I can't live without you."

There are hundreds of odd sayings, queer sentences, and peculiar words that are evidently making money for people. At least people continue to use them, and they get plenty of attention because of their humor or, perhaps, lack of humor – not because they are "magic words," but "word magic."

No collection of sales words would be complete without such sentences as these:

"Be the president of your own bank."
"The best book I ever owned." (Bank book advertisement.)
"Don't spend hours breaking your back. Let our washing

machine do it for you in one hour."

"Respectable dancing every day but Sunday."

"Marriages are made in heaven but wedding rings are made by us."

"Be your own boss."

"They laughed when I sat down to play."

"Do you make these mistakes in English?"

A Bronx beauty parlor, according to a recent statement by Walter Winchell, advertises:

"Permanent Wave – $3.00"

And a next-door rival counters with:

"Permanent Wave $5.00 – But Permanent"

**It is all in what you say and how you say it,
even in the Bronx!**

CHAPTER 28

A CIGARETTE GIRL CHANGES AN EXPRESSION AND INCREASES HER BUSINESS

> *"Cigars, cigarettes, and almonds" stops hotel guests.*
> *"Very hot chestnuts" clicks on Seventh Avenue and*
> *in Advertising Age. "The perambulating sandwich."*
> *Selling combs on Sixth Avenue.*

One day we were asked by the Hotels Statler chain to devise a new expression for its cigarette girls to use. It seemed, after some study on the subject, that "Cigars and cigarettes" failed to rouse people and crash through their cloud of thoughts, dreams, or conversations, as they sat in the restaurant.

People living next to a railroad soon fail to hear the train whistle. People in a hotel concentrate so much on their dining, conversation, or dancing that they fail to hear or see the little girl with her cigars and cigarettes.

Just to show you the power of changing a statement around ever so slightly, and gaining added results, we had the young lady in the Hotel Pennsylvania in New York City, as a test, say:

"Your CHOICE of cigars and cigarettes."

She would "Say It With Flowers" by holding a package of cigarettes in full view of the people sitting at their tables.

We also tried another simple "attention-getter" and "daze-crasher"

"Cigars, cigarettes, *and almonds.*"

Simple changes – but sales increased, because the young ladies received "renewed" attention with this new sales story that penetrated the haze!

There was a humorous twist to this last sentence, at least so I am told. It seems that up to twelve o'clock at night the girls would use the statement all right, but *after* twelve they would let down somewhat and say:

"Cigars, cigarettes, and almonds!"

And by three o'clock they were so tired that they would simply mutter, "Nuts and butts – nuts *and butts!*"

Anyway, this is a good story, illustrating our fifth principle:

It is all in HOW you say it, as well as in WHAT you say.

HOT CHESTNUTS FOR SALE

I saw an advertisement in *Advertising Age* endeavoring to show the importance of advertising properly. One of those fellows you see in the fall selling hot chestnuts on street corners was saying:

"Hot chestnuts."

His business was poor. The fellow down the street who was getting all of the business was saying: *"Very* hot chestnuts!"

One small five-and-ten-cent store conceived, some time ago, the idea of selling ice cream sandwiches in front of the store entrance. On the first warm day of the season, the manager had the porter bring the ice cream cooler outside, placed ice cream in it, and employed a pretty girl to sell it. You have seen these stands in front of many a five-and-ten-cent store. In this particular case, the sign was:

"The best ice cream sandwich in the city – 5¢."

It seemed that every year the ice cream business increased everywhere but in front of this store. A study of the situation showed that when a person bought a sandwich, he stood right there and ate it.

A PERAMBULATING SANDWICH

That was good advertising, at first, seeing people eat the ice cream, since it prompted other people to buy. But soon the entrance became so jammed that the shoppers could hardly get into the store, and many turned away because of that fact. To keep traffic moving *away* from the store entrance, yet to sell ice cream sandwiches, was really a problem for the store manager. One day, however, it was solved by giving the sandwich a name. What do you suppose the name was? It was *"Walk Away* Sandwich."

And people, realizing they could eat *and walk,* did walk away, leaving room for other shoppers to step up to the little counter in the store entrance and purchase sandwiches.

Three action words – that got action!

THE STORY OF THE COMB

One of those salesmen who fail to realize that the word "you" comes before "I," even in the word "business," was reciting a long-winded conversation about combs on a street corner. He hadn't heard about the rule, "Don't Write – Telegraph!" He was telling his small audience that the combs would "last a lifetime," would "massage the scalp," and would "never break, bend, or bust."

He did "Say It with Flowers," however, by pounding the comb on his stand. He would hit it with a hammer! Very dramatic, to be sure! Yet he failed to find the "sizzle," and so sold few combs. He said that the comb would do about all that any comb would be expected to do, yet he missed the main purpose, or "sizzle," until a quiet little fellow, quite innocently, from the back row of a small crowd said one day:

"But, tell me, sir, *will it comb the hair?*"

Don't, DON'T become so fancy with your verbiage that you miss the simple selling point. Don't put so much sauce on top of the steak that you kill the flavor. Sell the "sizzle" – not the trimmings.

The "sizzle" is MORE IMPORTANT than the cow!

A little newsboy selling a nationally known weekly magazine gets the immediate attention of women with this "door-crasher":

"Do you like good stories, madam?"

What woman can say "No" to that door approach!

"Sooey," says John Caples, is the simple word to call hogs to their suppers. "Sooey" – one word – but the RIGHT word!

FIND THE "SIZZLES"

Sometimes you are so close to your business, to your life, that you fail to see the "sizzles," the "square clothespins." You need somebody to point them out to you.

A mountaineer built his home with his front porch away from the cliff, paying no attention to the view of the whole valley below. He was so used to the good view in his "back yard" that he *didn't see* it any more.

A one-armed salesman approaches stenographers in offices with this question:

"Do you have use for a machine gun around here?"

"Of course not," says the astonished girl, sitting back, giving him her full attention, wondering why he said what he did.

With the complete attention of his prospect in ten seconds, the one-armed man holds up some pencils and says: *"Then perhaps you could use a good pencil!"*

But again BEWARE – don't use obvious tricks! They boomerang!

Don't help the customer say "No" by such statements as these:

"Is there anything else?"
"Something else today?"
"Will that be all?"

Word your questions so that it is impossible for the other person to respond with the two-letter negative, "No!" Try saying:

"What else?"

The other person begins to think, "What else do I need?" He can't say "No" to "What else?"

Of course, where possible, tell some ten-second story about some item you want to sell, and by selling the sizzle and not the steak, the bubbles and not the wine, the whiff and not the coffee, the pucker and not the pickle, your chances of making that extra sale are greater.

"Corns gone in five days or your money back," is a famous old headliner that is tested. What else can you say? It comes

189

out in ten short seconds; you "Say It With Flowers" with a guarantee. What a "sizzle" to a person with corns!

Selling the other person is so simple. Why make it complicated? Remember:

The selling word is mightier than the price tag.

CHAPTER 29

EIGHT LITTLE WORDS THAT
FOILED SOUVENIR HUNTERS

How a hotel stopped its guests' practice of removing pictures from the walls of the rooms – and thus saved its profits.

This is a short, simple story recently passed on to me by a former hotel man, who asked me not to mention his name. Knowing of our research into ways and means of making the contact between hotel employee and guest one of greater refinement, he thought this story would interest me.

It seems that this Midwestern hotel man hit upon an idea to keep "art lovers" from packing the pictures on the walls of the rooms into their trunks and suitcases before leaving the hotel.

People have a "souvenir complex" that prompts them to carry mementoes away with them, in memory of good times. These people are hard to deal with, and every hotel man worries about them. He knows he cannot come right out and say, "I believe one of our pictures is in your suitcase by mistake, madam." This would be embarrassing to the person. Besides, she might spend many hundreds of dollars in the hotel every year, and what is a $2.50 wall picture compared to that money! It is the constant trouble of replacing the pictures that annoys many a hotel manager. It is a source of petty irritation.

This problem has always remained unsolved – that is, until this Midwestern hotel man appeared in a store specializing in pictures for commercial use and ordered $11.00 pictures instead of the usual $2.50 ones.

"How does it happen," asked the salesman, "you are not reordering on the $2.50 ones you used to buy?"

"Because," was the answer, "guests used to take them from the walls. Our room rate is $2.50 a day, so it usually left us with no profit. We began to do some tall thinking. We struck upon this idea, all in eight little words. Now when a guest takes a picture from the wall, he finds a blank space with bright red lettering saying:

"A picture has been taken from this wall."

CHAPTER 30

TESTED WAYS TO HIRE – OR BE HIRED

> *What an executive looks for in an applicant. What an applicant looks for in an employer.*

Recently, the New York Sales Executives' Club asked me to make a study of the present-day methods of getting a job to get first-hand facts on what the job-seeker should do and say and what the executive looks for in a job-hunter.

This study was made with the able assistance of Mr. A. W. Morrison, sales manager for the McGraw-Hill Publishing Company, and Mr. Warren Rishel, president of Metal Products Exhibits, Inc.

We analyzed hundreds of case histories, and delved into the files of the Sales Club's own Man Marketing Clinic that meets weekly to diagnose the good and bad points of men needing work and to build a plan to help them "merchandise" themselves.

FOUR RULES LAID OUT

The same principles that make people buy shirts, neckties, rowboats, and automobiles, we found, make executives hire certain manpower to run their organizations, and can be used by the job-hunter to get himself suitable employment.

The four tested rules for getting a job are:

1. Watch your ten-second approach.
2. Have "You-Ability."
3. Have "Mesh-Ability."
4. Have "Close-Ability."

Our case histories showed that many employers judge the applicant during the first ten seconds. He catches a flash of the man's appearance, his personality, and is or is not impressed by his first ten words.

Snap judgments still rule the world, unfortunately! Therefore, the successful job-hunter will watch his opening statements.

DEFINITION OF "YOU-ABILITY"

"You-Ability" is an applicant's ability to get across to the executive's side of the desk *quickly* and *early* in the interview. Using the word "you" instead of "I" is one method of getting across to the executive's side of the desk, as in selling a product.

"Mesh-Ability" is an applicant's ability to "mesh his gears" with the thoughts and "thinking gears" running in the mind of the employer, and later when he has the job, to mesh gears with the policies of the organization and the personnel.

"Close-Ability," naturally, is the ability to close the interview in a dignified manner that is not embarrassing to either party. The discussion of salaries is always embarrassing to both parties, we found, if not handled diplomatically. If you have "Close-Ability," you will be hired quicker.

"PROFESSIONAL" JOB-HUNTERS

Incidentally, several interesting factors were brought out in this study of how to hire or be hired, among which was the discovery that there is a certain type of floating job-hunter who has perfected his technique so cleverly that he is an "experienced job-hunter." He uses his own "Tested Techniques" and "Tested Selling Sentences" to get the job, which he usually cannot hold. He puts on his best Sunday clothes, has a smile that can be turned on or shut off at will, and he knows all the answers to the usual questions in the mind of the executive. He is a "battle scarred" job seeker, well versed in what to say and do *in front of an employer.*

The following skit, which dramatically shows you the words and techniques to use if you are looking for a job, was drawn up and acted at a meeting of the Sales Executives' Club. Preceding the skit was a ten-minute talk by Frank Lovejoy, Standard Oil executive, and Sidney Edlund, president of Life Savers Corporation.

Read this skit and watch how Mr. Perennial Job-hunter loses out early in his interview, after making a flashing entrance with a personality "turned on" in a stupendous fashion. He makes many errors. One is that of trying to gain the sympathy of the boss by telling him about his personal troubles.

Then read how Mr. Do-It-Right handles his job-hunting interview, quickly gets his prospective employer interested, gets on the employer's side of the desk in short order, and lands the job.

HOW TO HIRE – OR BE HIRED

What an Executive Looks for in an Applicant –
What an Applicant Looks for in an Employer.

By

A. W. Morrison, Warren K. Rishel, and Elmer Wheeler

A Dramatic Skit for The New York Sales Executives' Club

Presented Monday, April 19, 1937

ACT I

What Employers Should Beware of –
or How Not to Get a Job

Scene: Office of Service Corporation of America. Any company that sells an intangible to the public.

Mr. Morrison: Master of Ceremonies, and the "Invisible Thoughts of the Executive."

Mr. Rishel: The typical American Executive.

Mr. Wheeler: Mr. Perennial Job-hunter, the battle-scarred job-hunter, who knows all the answers, in Act I; and Mr. Do-It-Right, in Act II.

Mr. Rishel is seated at his desk. The telephone rings. Mr. Rishel answers.

MR. RISHEL: "Hello. Someone about a job? Why I don't have any jobs open. Oh, the District Assemblyman sent him over. Well, let him in then."

MR. JOB-HUNTER: "My name is Job-hunter, *Perennial* Job-hunter. I used to be connected with the Whoosit Cracker Company, the What's-In-It Beer Company, and the Friday Fish Distributors."

MR. RISHEL: "Well–"

MR. JOB-HUNTER: "Well, I needa job real bad, Mr. Rishel.

"Haven't been working now for the past year or so and I've got a lot of debts piling up. The other day I was having a few beers with Pete Murphy, *your Assemblyman,* and he sez I should use his name and see you about a job. How ya fixed for jobs these days?"

MR. RISHEL: "Well, we're fixed pretty well around here. How are you and Murphy fixed?"

MR. JOB-HUNTER: "Well, you see I've had a lot of good jobs in my time, but I don't seem to get the right breaks, but I got some good testimonial letters.

"Here's a letter I got from the Whoosit Cracker Company. They let me out to make room for the boss's college son.

"Here is one from the What's-In-It Beer Company. They let me out because my boss and me got drunk after a sales convention, and the boss was scared to have me around after that.

"Now here's another letter from my last employer, the Friday Fish Distributing Corporation. I was just too big for that job!"

(Rishel reads testimonial letter.)

MR. RISHEL: "You say you were too big for this job?"

MR. JOB-HUNTER: "Yeah, too much office politics. The boss wouldn't listen to me. They're on the way out."

MR. RISHEL: "Humph! How long were you with them?"

MR. JOB-HUNTER: "Oh, three weeks was *enough* for me."

MR. RISHEL: "And that's *enough* FOR ME! Thanks for coming in."

MR. JOB-HUNTER: "Well, keep my name on file. Let me know when you have a good opening." (Leaving, says to himself.) "And they say the depression is over!"

ACT II

What Employers Should Look For –
or How to Get a Job

Scene: The same.

Mr. Rishel: The same typical American employer.

Mr. Wheeler: As himself.

Mr. Morrison: As the "Invisible Thoughts of the Employer."

(Makes use of charts back of employer, showing what is on employer's mind.)

The telephone rings. Mr. Rishel answers.

MR. RISHEL: "Hello. Mr. Do-It-Right? He has a dealer plan for me? Well, let him in."

MR. WHEELER: "Mr. Rishel?" (Extends hand.)

MR. RISHEL: "What is your name?"

MR. WHEELER: "Do-It-Right!"

MR. RISHEL: "Mr. Right?"

MR. WHEELER: "Right!"

MR. RISHEL: "What can I do for you?"

MR. WHEELER: "Mr. Rishel, as I told your secretary, I have a dealer plan which not only will be helpful in solving some of your dealer problems, but will be helpful to me."

MR. RISHEL: "What do you know about *my* problems?"

MR. WHEELER: "Fundamentally, *all* dealer selling problems are about the same. Aren't they, Mr. Rishel?"

MR. RISHEL: "Yes – but we've got our own headaches. Our proposition is different!"

MR. WHEELER: "Of course, Mr. Rishel, each product or service has its individual peculiarities.

"But what would you say some of *your own* individual headaches were?"

MR. RISHEL: "Our biggest headache is to get the dealer to carry through."

MR. WHEELER: "Mr. Rishel, you'll no doubt be interested in how the Always Progressive Corporation met that problem."

MR. RISHEL: "Well, how did they?"

MR. WHEELER: "They put us to work *with* their dealers, not *on* them!"

MR. RISHEL: *"With* their dealers, not *on* them! Hmm! That's well expressed, young man. How was it done?"

MR. WHEELER: "First we made a study of the dealer's problems. This was done right in his *own* store, behind his *own* counters, on his *own* customers. We made three important discoveries which I have briefly listed in this recommendation for your business." (Hands proposal to Rishel.)

MR. RISHEL: "In other words, you helped the dealer help himself – and he naturally bought from you?"

MR. WHEELER: "Yes, Sir. You see the best products won't sell themselves – and the best-looking dotted line won't sign *itself.*

"We realized, as salesmen, that our job really began AFTER we got our goods on the dealer's shelf. We had to help him move the goods off the shelf, by showing him certain TESTED selling methods that make people buy.

"We worked *with* the dealer – not *on* the dealer."

MR. RISHEL: (Getting interested.) "Could this sales training job of working *with* the dealer be done in my business? You know it's different from others."

MR. WHEELER: "As long as your salesmen must say *something* to your dealers, and as long as the dealers must *say something* to the public in selling your services, you can use this TESTED plan of teaching dealers WHAT to say and HOW to say it."

MR. RISHEL: "Well, we certainly use words and sales processes in our business – but what assurance can you give me that this novel plan will work with us? We are different, you know, and I must have some proof to give our president."

MR. WHEELER: "Have you a territory in such bad shape that

you are not afraid to experiment?"

MR. RISHEL: "You're right, I have – I have one that *nothing* could make worse."

MR. WHEELER: "All right, Mr. Rishel, assign me that territory, pay my expenses and a reasonable percentage on results, *and I'll rest my case on performance.*"

MR. RISHEL: "When would you be able to start?"

MR. WHEELER: "Well, I would like to give my present employer a little time. Say – one month!"

MR. RISHEL: "Let's go into the president's office!"

Summed up, the four things to remember if you are to hire or to be hired, are:

1. The ten-second approach
2. "You-Ability"
3. "Mesh-Ability"
4. "Close-Ability"

Whether you are selling a tangible or an intangible, a piece of actual merchandise *or yourself,* a human cargo, you will find that knowledge of TESTED words and TESTED selling techniques will be important. Words carry your thoughts. You can send your thoughts out on an old-fashioned steam engine or send them forth on a streamlined train.

Streamlined trains go faster – and farther! Use them!

CHAPTER 31

THE CIGAR-STORE INDIAN
NEVER MADE A SALE

All the cigar-store Indian did was attract people to the store. A live clerk inside had to make the actual sale. Many a salesman is a wooden Indian and doesn't know it. The Automat is the only place to date where you can drop coins into slots and get waited on. But even the Automat can't "trade-up," sell "extra items," or make "multiple" sales.

An insurance salesman got into my office the other day and asked, "Who is your worst enemy?" This took me off my feet. I knew he was prospecting for "leads," but insurance salesmen usually want names of friends, relatives, or acquaintances. This man wanted my "worst enemies."

When I asked him why, he explained that he received too much resistance when he asked for names of friends. People do not want to have salesmen calling on their friends. He hit upon the "worst-enemy" angle, and he tells me it works!

A favorite way, if you are a life insurance salesman, to get the prospect talking is to ask leading questions, such as "Are you married?" – "Have any children?" – "Are they boys or girls?" – "How old are they?" The prospect finds himself responding to these questions, warming himself up, and at the same time giving needed information to the salesman.

A GOOD LEADING QUESTION

Another insurance salesman finds this to be his favorite leading question, "What is the thing you'd like most to give your children if something happened to you?"

Most men say, "A million dollars," and this salesman shakes his head slowly, saying, "That would be the worst thing you could do – it would ruin them! What you would like to leave your children would be the FULL TIME of their mother, with no financial worries, so that she could help them become the fine people you would like them to be."

Whenever a sale is slipping, another insurance salesman uses this "Tested Selling Sentence" to get his prospect coming after the "bait." He says, "How long is it since you have had your blood pressure taken?" And then, "Do you think you could pass this examination?" This reflection on his health will challenge many a man.

It takes a "live wire," not a wooden Indian, to know when and how to use these "power words" effectively and make people respond, especially when they ask the age-old question on seeing several different pieces of merchandise or sales packages, "What's the difference?"

A book salesman came into my office the other day. I told him I was too busy at the moment to talk with him, and he said, "I know you are busy – I call only on busy people!" He received my full attention.

The old-fashioned statement, "Miss, is your mother home?" has worked successfully on many a doorstep, and you may be surprised to learn that it is still being used, and rather successfully too, on the newer generation. Often one word makes or breaks a sale, so weigh your words carefully *before,* not after, you use them.

THE HOLLYWOOD CASTING OFFICE

It is the little things you say and do that put you across. Realizing this, the main casting office in Hollywood has abandoned the old statement to people calling up for assignments, "Nothing today," and have substituted the words, "Call tomorrow."

I am told that this simple change in language is giving hope to many people who must call up, day after day, for assignments, and that the number of suicides was lessened by these two encouraging words, "Call tomorrow," instead of the pessimistic "Nothing today."

It is not a pleasant thing to talk about "feet," but it is quite proper to talk about your "foot."

Back in the days when Niagara Falls was the favorite place for newlyweds, there were leather wall pieces with pictures of Indians, dogs, beautiful girls, and other things being sold to the tourists. You perhaps have seen one of these leather pieces hanging in your grandparents' home.

One of them showed the picture of a dog with the inscription, "He won't bite you." This particular picture was a poor seller until one day the inscription was changed to, "All I do is growl a little." Sales tripled. The word "bite" in the poor seller evidently brought up a negative thought. Besides, the first caption was not as personal as the second, which was the dog's own words, theoretically.

Henry Ford changed a billboard headline from "Buy a Ford

and *Bank* the difference" to "Buy a Ford and *Spend* the difference," and gained added goodwill from the merchants.

Watch your words. Look out for the wag behind what you say. Watch your bark.

THE BEGGAR USES TESTED SELLING

Last spring in Central Park I noticed a blind man with an unusual sign that stated, "It's spring – and I am blind." Many were the coins dropped into his hand.

A salesman who isn't a wooden Indian visits farmers to sell them implements. His usual approach to new prospects is, "How would you like to have a new cow every year?" The farmers always rest on their plows and inquire, "How?" Then they receive the sales story.

When I finished my recent address before the International Stewards' and Caterers' Convention in Philadelphia, the Anheuser-Busch representative from Texas stated he had difficulty selling beer in bottles in that state. He informed me that the young people ordered beer in glasses, and while they danced the beer went "dead," and the drinking places got complaints. He told me he would try using "Tested Selling Sentences" and would change the words, "Draught or bottle beer?" to merely, "Bottle beer?" He felt that this would prompt people to buy beer in bottles which could be left unopened until ready for drinking. I think he is right. I think he has a mighty good "sizzle" for his dealers.

"Just add water," is mighty important to the sale of several products.

Good sales words must be simple and clothed in "inno-cence" to work effectively, for once you recognize that you are being sold with a sales talk, you will close your reasoning and become a poor prospect.

CHAPTER 32

SUMMARY OF THE FIVE WHEELERPOINTS

During these years of building the world's first and only Word Laboratory wherein sales talks are manufactured and then tested, I have often been asked for our formula in putting words together with their techniques into sales presentations, and for the first time in this book I have given you these principles. Let's review them quickly:

WHEELERPOINT 1
DON'T SELL THE STEAK – SELL THE SIZZLE!

The sizzle has sold more steaks than the cow ever has, although the cow is, of course, mighty important. Hidden in everything you sell are "sizzles." The "sizzle" is the best selling argument. It's the bubble in the wine; the tang in the cheese; the whiff in the coffee.

Look for the "sizzles" in your sales package and use them first to get the sale started – so you have a chance to follow through.

The first thing the prospect asks himself about what you are selling is, "What will it do for me?" You must put on a pair of "sizzle glasses" and look at your product through his eyes so you can answer this big question.

Being able to say "you" instead of "I" is what I call "YOU-ABILITY." By developing "You-ability" you soon learn how to find "sizzles" and how to fit them to each prospect in tailor-made fashion – and in the order that the prospect, not you, considers important!

A little old woman was looking at stoves. A salesman with a "canned" talk but no regard for his prospect started at the bottom of the stove and outlined each and every "sizzle" to his prospect. He told her about the good paint job; how the stove was high enough to permit a dog to sleep under it; how the enamel wouldn't chip; how fine cakes and pies could be baked. When he was finally exhausted, the little old woman asked sweetly and simply:

"But will it keep a little old lady warm?"

The rule to remember is this:

What is a "sizzle" to one person may be a "fizzle" or a whole bonfire to another person. Therefore, fit the "sizzle" to the prospect on hand!

WHEELERPOINT 2
"DON'T WRITE – TELEGRAPH"

By this I mean, get the prospect's IMMEDIATE and FAVORABLE attention in the fewest possible words. Your first ten words are more important than your next ten thousand – for you have only ten short seconds to catch the fleeting interest of the other person, and, if your first message doesn't "click," the prospect leaves you mentally – if not physically!

Therefore, the second rule for a successful presentation with "Tested Selling Sentences" is to make every word count by using "telegraphic" statements, because you don't have time for long "letters."

People form snap judgments and make up their opinions about you during the first ten seconds. Their first judgment affects their entire attitude toward what you are selling.

When you face your prospect don't guess and gamble – don't stammer and stutter – don't hem and haw! Know what you are going to say and do. Be sure it is "TESTED!" The rule to keep in mind is this: *It's all in what you say the first ten seconds!*

If you apply this simple rule, the technique that goes with what you say will come naturally to you in Wheelerpoint 3.

WHEELERPOINT 3
"SAY IT WITH FLOWERS"

This simply means, PROVE your statements. Give a quick customer benefit – but then prove it the next second. "Happy returns of the day" when accompanied with flowers proves you MEAN it.

You have only ten short seconds and two able hands to sell the prospect – so fortify your words with performance; back up your selling "sizzles" with showmanship!

Your words will get much better results if SUPPORTED with action than if left hanging mid-air to themselves, no matter how good the words may be.

You all know how little the perfunctory "Thank you" of some clerks means to you. It lacks the reinforcement of sincerity.

It's the little things you DO as you speak your lines that make the sales presentation stand out. The movement of your hands – your head – your feet – tells the prospect how sincere and honest you are.

Don't be a "comic valentine" salesman with a shine in your sales talk and bags in your selling technique as well as in your pants. Don't be the telegraph operator who knows the message but fumbles the keys.

Make the wires sing out – but make them sing DRAMAT-ICALLY.

Get action with action!

Demonstrate – but DEMONSTRATE TO SELL!

Synchronize your "sizzles" with SHOWMANSHIP!

The motion that accompanies utterance of words – the expression on the seller's face at the time – the manner in which he handles the product – all are a part of a successful presentation with "Tested Selling."

The rule for you to apply is this: *Say the "sizzle" quickly – but say it with gestures!*

And then when the time comes to stop your parade of "sizzles" and ask the prospect to buy, use the principles in the next Wheelerpoint.

WHEELERPOINT 4
DON'T ASK IF – ASK WHICH!

We mean you should always frame your words (especially at the close) so that you give the prospect a choice between something and SOMETHING, never between something and NOTHING.

Ask leading questions like the good lawyer – but always ask a question that gets the answer YOU want! Never take a chance and ask a question unless you know the reply you will get.

There are two kinds of salesmen, those who talk with question marks and those who talk with exclamation marks. Be the question-mark salesman who hooks his prospect's interest with leading questions – do not whack him into submission with exclamation marks.

Never ask the prospect *if* he wants to buy – but WHICH! Give him a choice. Ask him what, when, where, or how much he wants to buy. Not if – but which!

Ask the right question and you'll get the answer YOU want!

"Tested Questions" revive wavering sales. Whenever you feel the sale slipping, ask a question that starts you off on a new tack. A "Tested Question" gives you a breathing spell while the prospect answers.

The word "why" is the hardest single word in the English language and in a salesman's vocabulary for an objecting prospect to answer. Use the word "why" whenever the prospect objects. Watch him wiggle trying to put phantom objections into words that answer your "why."

Try this "why" system at home. The next time the wife asks for a new hat, politely ask her, "Why do you want one?" Watch her struggle to give you reasons, which are usually so silly she doesn't want to tell them to you.

During the depression you found it necessary to say "No" because you had little money with which to say "Yes." The depression may be over, but from force of habit you still say "No," unless a clever salesman makes the "No" *difficult* to say.

The rule to remember is this: *You can catch more fish with hooks than with crowbars.*

Now with these four important selling points in mind, there is still one more necessary to the making of a successful sales presentation.

WHEELERPOINT 5
WATCH YOUR BARK!

Consider how much the little dog can express with just ONE WORD and ONE TAIL to wag. What he does with the tone of his "woof" and the wag of his tail to convey his many messages to you is well worth emulating.

Watch the bark that can creep into your voice – watch the "wag" behind your words. This is the fifth and final element of a successful "Tested Selling" presentation.

The finest "sizzle" that you "telegraph" in ten seconds, with huge bouquets of "flowers" and lots of "which," "whom," "where," and "how," will flop if your voice is flat.

Don't be a Johnny-one-note. Train your voice to run its entire scale. Cup your hands behind your ears and hear yourself talk. Be a director who can play all the instruments. Avoid voice peculiarities. Have the voice with the smile, but not the smile that is automatically "turned on" for the immediate benefit of the prospect. Never smile insincerely like the wolf at Red Riding Hood's door.

Remember: The wooden Indian tattooed with selling words never sold a cigar. He merely brought customers into the store for a real, live-wire salesman to sell.

This fifth rule is simple: *It is all in how you say it and the way you say it as well as in what you say!*

If you will apply these five simple selling points, you will find that your sales will be more accurate, more foolproof, and faster – for these five principles come fresh off the firing line, and are TESTED to make people respond to your way of thinking.

We told you how when the Johns-Manville Housing Guild

salesmen approach their prospects on front porches in cold canvass calls, their opening "Tested Selling Sentence" is "Here is your FREE copy of *101 Ways to Improve Your Home.*" This is how they solve the screen-door problem!

We told you how the Texas Company used a single "Tested Selling Sentence" to introduce their New Texaco Oil two years ago, and their 45,000 dealers got under 250,000 hoods in one week's time – exposing themselves to this much business!

We told you how Mr. H. W. Hoover knows that the finest idea on his Hoover cleaner will be accepted as matter-of-fact by women unless that idea is dramatized in words that blaze themselves effectively across the minds of the prospects, and so each Hoover selling statement must be (1) easy to speak, and (2) have remembrance value.

Therefore, the signal that tells the woman the bag needs cleaning is not called a "danger device" but the "Time-to-Empty Signal," and the salesman says: "You may forget to clean the bag, but this new Hoover won't forget to remind you." The headlight is called the "Dirt Finder," and the "Tested Statement" that goes with this colorful description is, "It sees where to clean, and it's clean where it's been."

We have found after analyzing 105,000 such word combinations and techniques as the above examples and having tested them on 19,000,000 people that the "canned" sales talk is not as effective as the "planned" sales talk which is made foolproof through intelligent pre-testing in the field under normal selling conditions, to make the statements scientifically defensible.

"WORD MAGIC" – NOT "MAGIC WORDS"

Now I have given you these five points, the result of ten

years' study of the sales words and techniques used by successful salespeople in many kinds of businesses, and you can apply
them to your own business.

Successful selling depends on many things, of course, but
after all, it is the words you use and the things you do as you
stand face to face with your prospect that make or break the
sale for you.

There are no such things as "magic words." But there is
"word magic!"

"Tested Selling Sentences" are never "high-pressure" or
"canned" statements – we do not recommend either – but are
well-chosen sentences designed to give the prospect the necessary information in an acceptable manner so that he or she can
easily and naturally reach the conclusion YOU aim for.

In every buyer's mind there is always a "dream" and a
"need" whenever he is making a purchase of any consequence.
The *first* thing the seller should do is satisfy the "dream"
desire, and second, fill the "need." The "sizzle" stimulates as
well as satisfies the "desire," but be sure the "steak" came from
the right part of a good "steer" or the reaction will be disap-
pointment.

A $20,000 automobile will stop if a 10¢ gas connection
fails. A business will stop if the salesman fails to say and do
the right thing at the right time.

A chain with one link holding fifty pounds, another sixty
pounds, and a third three pounds is only as strong as the
"pulling power" of the three-pound link, and so it is with your
business; it is only as strong as the selling power of your salesmen.

What your salesmen do on the firing line, whether it be on
front and back porches, or behind selling counters, or in busi-

ness offices, determines the amount of smoke that comes out of your factory chimneys. This smoke is in direct PROPORTION to the salesmanship of your selling force!

Summed up, the philosophy behind "Tested Selling" is this:

"Don't think so much about what you want to say, as about what the prospect wants to hear – then the response you will get will more often be the one you are aiming for."

THE END

TELL ME
WHAT
YOU THINK!

I am thrilled to hear what you think about **Tested Sentences That Sell by Elmer Wheeler**. Please feel free to share your comments, feedback and/or suggestions on the form below, tear it out, and mail it to: BMC, PO Box 102935, Denver, CO 80250. **Thank you!**

I hereby freely allow and give right to the publisher or their associates, to use the following comments, feedback and suggestions either to improve this book or use in any advertising medium determined by the publisher.

_____

Your Signature   Date

_____

_____

_____

_____

_____

This Certificate Entitles Bearer To A Free Copy of "8 Tested Selling Power Principles" by Elmer Wheeler

(The First 8 Chapters of *Tested Sentences That Sell*)

This Certificate is From:

Full Name: _____

Postal Address: _____

City: _____ State: _____

Zip: _____ Country: _____

And is Presented To:

Full Name: _____

Postal Address: _____

City: _____ State: _____

Zip: _____ Country: _____

Redemption Instructions:

Via the Internet:

Visit **www.TestedSelling.com/freebook** and follow the redemption instructions.

Via postal mail:

Legibly complete the above form and mail to: Free "Tested Sentences" Offer, BMC, PO Box 102935, Denver, CO 80250. All fields must be complete and accurate.

Your free book should arrive within 2-6 weeks. Valid while supplies last.

This Certificate Entitles Bearer To A Free Copy of "8 Tested Selling Power Principles" by Elmer Wheeler

(The First 8 Chapters of *Tested Sentences That Sell*)

This Certificate is From:

Full Name: _____

Postal Address: _____

City: _____ State: _____

Zip: _____ Country: _____

And is Presented To:

Full Name: _____

Postal Address: _____

City: _____ State: _____

Zip: _____ Country: _____

Redemption Instructions:

Via the Internet:

Visit **www.TestedSelling.com/freebook** and follow the redemption instructions.

Via postal mail:

Legibly complete the above form and mail to: Free "Tested Sentences" Offer, BMC, PO Box 102935, Denver, CO 80250. All fields must be complete and accurate.

Your free book should arrive within 2-6 weeks. Valid while supplies last.

This Certificate Entitles Bearer To A Free Copy of "8 Tested Selling Power Principles" by Elmer Wheeler

(The First 8 Chapters of *Tested Sentences That Sell*)

This Certificate is From:

Full Name: _____

Postal Address: _____

City: _____ State: _____

Zip: _____ Country: _____

And is Presented To:

Full Name: _____

Postal Address: _____

City: _____ State: _____

Zip: _____ Country: _____

Redemption Instructions:

Via the Internet:

Visit **www.TestedSelling.com/freebook** and follow the redemption instructions.

Via postal mail:

Legibly complete the above form and mail to: Free "Tested Sentences" Offer, BMC, PO Box 102935, Denver, CO 80250. All fields must be complete and accurate.

Your free book should arrive within 2-6 weeks. Valid while supplies last.

This Certificate Entitles Bearer To A Free Copy of *"8 Tested Selling Power Principles"* by *Elmer Wheeler*

(The First 8 Chapters of *Tested Sentences That Sell*)

This Certificate is From:

Full Name: _____

Postal Address: _____

City: _____ State: _____

Zip: _____ Country: _____

And is Presented To:

Full Name: _____

Postal Address: _____

City: _____ State: _____

Zip: _____ Country: _____

Redemption Instructions:

Via the Internet:

Visit **www.TestedSelling.com/freebook** and follow the redemption instructions.

Via postal mail:

Legibly complete the above form and mail to: Free "Tested Sentences" Offer, BMC, PO Box 102935, Denver, CO 80250. All fields must be complete and accurate.

Your free book should arrive within 2-6 weeks. Valid while supplies last.

This Certificate Entitles Bearer To A Free Copy of *"8 Tested Selling Power Principles"* by Elmer Wheeler

(The First 8 Chapters of *Tested Sentences That Sell*)

This Certificate is From:

Full Name: _____

Postal Address: _____

City: _____ State: _____

Zip: _____ Country: _____

And is Presented To:

Full Name: _____

Postal Address: _____

City: _____ State: _____

Zip: _____ Country: _____

Redemption Instructions:

Via the Internet:

Visit **www.TestedSelling.com/freebook** and follow the redemption instructions.

Via postal mail:

Legibly complete the above form and mail to: Free "Tested Sentences" Offer, BMC, PO Box 102935, Denver, CO 80250. All fields must be complete and accurate.

Your free book should arrive within 2-6 weeks. Valid while supplies last.

CPSIA information can be obtained at www.ICGtesting.com
Printed in the USA
BVOW02s2222230114

342895BV00010B/519/P